Afro-American Poetics

Revisions of Harlem and the Black Aesthetic

HOUSTON A. BAKER, Jr.

THE UNIVERSITY OF WISCONSIN PRESS

The University of Wisconsin Press
114 North Murray Street
Madison, Wisconsin 53715

The University of Wisconsin Press, Ltd.
1 Gower Street
London WC1E 6HA, England

5   4   3   2
Printed in the United States of America

Photographic credits: Jean Toomer (p. 18) and Amiri Baraka
(p. 116), courtesy of the Moorland-Spingarn Research Center,
Howard University, Washington, D.C.; Countee Cullen (p. 50),
courtesy of the estate of Carl Van Vechten, Joseph Solomon,
executor; Larry Neal (p. 146), photograph by Roy Lewis; and
Hoyt Fuller (p. 163), courtesy of Abena Joan Brown.

Library of Congress Cataloging-in-Publication Data
Baker, Houston A.
   Afro-American poetics : revisions of Harlem and the Black
aesthetic / Houston A. Baker, Jr.
      212 pp.   cm.
   Includes bibliographical references and index.
   ISBN 0-299-11500-3
      1. American literature — Afro-American authors — History and
criticism. 2. American literature — 20th century — History and
criticism. 3. Afro-Americans in literature. 4. Afro-Americans —
Aesthetics. 5. Harlem Renaissance. I. Title. II. Title:
Afroamerican poetics.
PS153.N5B22   1988   88-2724
810'.9'896073 — dc19   CIP

Afro-American Poetics

This work is dedicated to the memory of
Hoyt W. Fuller (1923–1983)

Contents

Acknowledgments

I wish to thank those who supported earlier appearances of various portions of the present work. First, I extend my gratitude to Phil Petrie and the Howard University Press for *Singers of Daybreak,* a 1974 collection of critical essays in which "Journey Toward Black Art: Jean Toomer's *Cane*" first appeared. The now defunct Broadside Press Critics Series originally published my reflections on Countee Cullen as *A Many-Colored Coat of Dreams: The Poetry of Countee Cullen* (1974). The now defunct *Minority Voices* first published " 'These are songs if you have the / music': An Essay on Imamu Baraka" (1977). And *Callaloo* originally printed "Critical Change and Blues Continuity: An Essay on the Criticism of Larry Neal" (1985).

The present fashion in acknowledgments is brevity, and I do not want to fly in the face of that convention. But I do want to extend gratitude to a *community* of scholars, critics, artists, and spokespersons of Afro-American expressive culture who helped me to what can only be called my "second birth" into blackness. This ever-expanding community not only gave me birth as a Black Aesthetician, but also nurtured me through the years. In its guise as "tradition" or "ancestral wisdom," it always enables any individual Afro-American scholar to say with the bluesman Buck MacFarland: "I was born black 'fore my birth." In addition to the community, there are people who must be thanked individually. Many thanks go to Sterling Brown, who has bequeathed an awesome legacy; to Gwendolyn Brooks, who has demonstrated how always to tell the truth; and especially to Hoyt W. Fuller, who forwarded a mighty work. Among younger members of the com-

munity, I want to thank Kimberly Benston and Henry Louis
Gates, Jr., for welcoming me into the circle of theoreticians. And
many thanks are due as well to Barbara Hanrahan for consistently
fine editorial support.

My greatest gratitude, as always, goes to my wife, Charlotte,
and my son, Mark, whose love and support are unfailing.

It goes without saying that I alone am responsible for all errors
in the following pages.

Philadelphia
January 1987

Afro-American Poetics

Introduction

Initially conceived as a collection of previously published essays, the present work encountered stony gazes from humanities editors whose sentiments echoed those of a French scholar who told me that collections of essays are the privilege of *les grands messieurs.* I can scarcely claim such a title. At the time the idea of a collection occurred to me, however, I had begun the reading, teaching, and lecturing that eventually embodied itself as *Modernism and the Harlem Renaissance.* [1] I had also begun to teach and lecture in the area of Afro-American women's writing — activities that led eventually to *Workings of the Spirit: The Poetics of Afro-American Women's Writing.* [2] Four years after my initial idea of a collection, I found myself engaged not by an array of fugitive essays but by the design of the second book in a critical trilogy.

Situating itself between my extended meditation on the discursive forms of the Harlem Renaissance and my attempt to articulate a poetics of Afro-American women's writing, the present book became a kind of intellectual autobiography. It is a chronicle of the journey that produced a specific critical orientation. "Our intellectual autobiographies are endlessly fascinating," said one of my colleagues, "but not necessarily to other people."

I do not consider the account that follows endlessly fascinating, but I believe it represents an important story in the history of American literary criticism. It presents the sound and self of a critical movement's emergence and progress and comprises a chapter in any "official" story of recent shifts in American literary study.

My story begins at the origin of all intellectual autobiography — with a prior text. The argument of *Modernism and the Harlem*

3

Renaissance implied the revised critical posture that marks the present work. I shall have more to say about that posture in due course. For the moment I want to give a brief account of the general argument of *Modernism and the Harlem Renaissance.*

The book suggests that a reassessment is required of the Harlem Renaissance—that moment in the 1920s when Afro-American intellectuals and artists were more plentiful and influential than ever before. Such a reassessment takes place in the book under the sign of a specifically Afro-American modernism. This modernism, I argue, was concerned preeminently with removing the majority of the black population from the poverty, illiteracy, and degradation that marked southern, black, agrarian existence in the United States at the turn of the nineteenth century. Afro-American scholars, intellectuals, and activists of the late nineteenth and early twentieth centuries were faced with a task substantially different from that of their Anglo-American, British, and Irish counterparts. Rather than bashing the bourgeoisie, such spokespersons were attempting to create one. Far from being rebellious dissenters against existent Afro-American expressive forms, they sought to enhance these forms and bring them before a sophisticated public. And far from repudiating the emergent age as "an old bitch gone in the teeth," Afro-American spokespersons welcomed a new century as a time when shackles of slavery and impoverishment would fall decisively away.

Only a discursive history of Afro-America from 1895 to, say, 1930 yields such an account of the Harlem twenties. By discursive history, I mean careful analysis of selected critical, polemical, and creative texts. What emerges from my own analyses of texts such as Booker T. Washington's *Up from Slavery,* W. E. B. DuBois's *The Souls of Black Folk,* and Alain Locke's *The New Negro* is far more akin to a racial epic than to an anecdotal account of the 1920s.

Washington, Locke, and DuBois agreed that the signal drama of the twentieth century was comprised by a "whole people"—a nation of Afro-Americans—coming to democratic birth. They considered expressive cultural forms such as African masks (Locke), black oratory or public speaking (Washington), and Afro-American spirituals (Locke and DuBois) signs of the imminence of such a birth. They thought of black expressive culture as a reservoir from which a quintessentially Afro-American spirit flowed. No matter how ineffable the source of this spirit or elusive its precise contours, it was a national spirit — an impulse, that is to say, which augured the birth of a nation perceptibly different from the one conceived by D. W. Griffith.[3]

The spirit evoked by the Afro-American modernists is an eternally transformative impulse that converts desire not only into resonant and frequently courageous sound but also into ceaseless motion. A picture arises of civil rights marchers moving into the very face of white viciousness, singing "Woke up this morning with my mind set on freedom." The stirring cadences of Martin Luther King, Jr., describing craggy mountaintops and bountiful plains of freedom resound in the background.

The national impulse valorized by Locke, DuBois, and Washington is best described, I believe, as Afro-American spirit work. It is a form of energy that Jean Toomer describes as "genius" in his beautiful book *Cane*.[4] The poem "Georgia Dusk," which occupies an important space in *Cane*, contains the following lines:

A feast of moon and men and barking hounds,
An orgy for some *genius* of the South
With blood-hot eyes and cane-lipped scented mouth,
Surprised in making folk-songs from soul sounds.

"Genius" can, indeed, be the process and product of a felicitous (surprising) transformation of racial soul sounds into a report from black vernacular valleys. It may consist also in the inventive creation of a critical or analytical model for capturing or sounding such transformations.

The resultant critical model might comprise, in fact, a kind of racial poetics. The discursive history of Afro-American modernism, as I conceive it, reveals the "spirit work" of a racial genius. It reveals, as well, a continuous attempt by Afro-American spokespeople such as Washington, DuBois, and Locke to attune themselves to this genius and to extend its forward motion.

My interpretation of the work of turn-of-the-century and Harlem Renaissance spokespeople in *Modernism and the Harlem Renaissance* attempts to move in accord with a racial genius figured forth by *Cane.* My interpretation takes for granted the always arbitrary character of historical plots. It assumes, in other words, that boundaries and prospects of any "period," "school," or "movement" defined by extant social or literary histories of Afro-America are contingent phenomena—products, undeniably, of what their authors classify as pertinent information, and what they reject as noise. *Spirit work,* or what I designated as "renaissancism" in *Modernism and the Harlem Renaissance,* can be read as an interpretive design, or, a historical "emplotment."[5] It is conceived as already in place and manifestly invented. It produces, I believe, a far less dismal story of the twenties than the one told by Nathan Huggins in his pioneering *Harlem Renaissance* and David Lewis in *When Harlem Was in Vogue.*[6] The raison d'être for what I consider my new emplotment of Afro-American expressive culture is revision. I want to revise stories like those of Huggins and Lewis as well as stories that I myself have told of the Harlem twenties and the Black Arts sixties. In the following pages, therefore, I attempt to refigure old boundaries and to create anew the contours of black expressive culture and criticism in the United States.

The process of writing a revisionary tale or countermyth is always twofold. Washington, Locke, and DuBois each added discursive possibilities, forms, and strategies to the field of Afro-American racial genius in their attempts to *discover* and forward what they considered already in place—Afro-American racial genius. Similarly, proponents of the Black Aesthetic *discovered* precursors such as Locke and DuBois and invented revisionary forms which they held to be in harmony with the existing spirit of such precursors. Black Aesthetic efforts were, thus, both reclamations and inventions. They rediscovered "Harlem" and added to its discursive field such expressive forms as the postmodernist chant poem marked by its *Anders-streben* toward the genius of John Coltrane and the oratory of Malcolm X. They also crafted striking revolutionary dramas like those of LeRoi Jones, Douglas Turner Ward, Ed Bullins, and others.

My revisionary project is also one of reclamation and invention. It denotes predecessors' forms such as those of the Harlem twenties and the Black Arts sixties. It also inventively connotes its own formal difference vis-à-vis previous interpretive accounts. The principal role in the story is occupied by a perduring *spirit work*. The story of spirit work is a unifying myth. It provides coherence for both the autobiographical self and the general Afro-American cultural enterprise described in the following pages. One might say that it is my own narrative for confronting the disappearance of culture and the self announced by postmodernism.

That is to say, my current project acknowledges the rhetorical character of categories such as "mankind," "self," "culture," and "other." At the same time, it recognizes that any prevalent rhetoric is a function of class-, race-, and gender-based access to the means of rhetorical production. Aware as I am that rhetoric makes uneasy kin of us all, I also realize that a greater access to such means makes some rhetoricians seem more kin than others. We are currently party to myths of a nonself because rhetoricians of this myth are privileged. One can, however, always refuse to be part of a deconstructionist collective.

By refusing to play the role of poor relation or workhorse to deconstruction, we can, perhaps, begin to insist on our allegiance to another family altogether. Rhetorical inventiveness and the secondariness to which language condemns human beings are not stunning revelations to African-Americans who have perennially found ourselves consigned to "sambo," "nigger," "chattel personal," "roving bands of Negro youth," "teenage mother," or "black family in crisis" in the master discourse. It has always been necessary for black people in America not only to comprehend the space of their identity-in-difference but also energetically to refigure this space by employing expressive counterenergy like that found in a recent rap: "You know I'm proud to be a black, Y'all / And that's a fact, Y'all / And if you try to take what's mine / I'll take it back, Y'all / It's like that!"[7]

Deconstruction — in the manner of most American philosophical musings since the origin of the thirteen colonies — looks eternally and wistfully abroad. It seeks a model of language's implications and culture's myriad contrived corridors from England or France. But the malaise of American nonselves and American cultural secondariness has its roots and seeks its explanation, not abroad, but on national shores. Afro-Americans — from Jamestown's first disembarkation of "twenty negres" to the era of Run-DMC—have been deconstructionists par excellence. They have continuously shaken (or solicited) Western discourse with *spirit work*.

My intention in the following pages has been determinately rhetorical. I have endeavored to rewrite familiar definitions of Afro-American expressive culture not only by recontextualizing earlier scholarly interpretations (my own included) but also by writing my self-in-motion as part of this revisionist enterprise. My revised critical project, therefore, comes to signify me (and on me) in the same way that "tradition" or "deconstruction" writes both a creative practice and the practicing traditional or deconstructionist critic. The import of my own myth of cultural coherence, therefore, can be stated as a hypothesis about critical practice in general: *Critics eternally become and embody the generative myths of their culture by half-perceiving and half-inventing their culture, their myths, and themselves.*

What remains to be addressed is the always legitimate question that confronts any collection of previously published work: "Why?" A partial answer is implicit in my foregoing remarks. A more complete response includes some account of institutional matters surrounding American publishing. My critical and creative efforts share with the work of my Afro-American brothers, sisters, and ancestors the distinction of having been rejected by some of the very best publishing outlets in the United States. Traditionally, what are called first-rate publishers, journals, and reviews in the United States have not hastened to solicit or issue works by or devoted to black people. Hence we have been compelled, when *PMLA* or *American Literature* said "No," to seek other agencies for the dissemination of our ideas.

In earlier decades—as the Cornell University Black Periodical Fiction Project has revealed—our outlets were newspapers and club and church periodicals. In recent years, we established similar journals, presses, and even bookstores of our own. These ventures were usually undercapitalized, and many enjoyed but a fleeting life.

Having experienced a kind of "second birth" when I began teaching Afro-American literature, I eagerly enlisted in the ranks of the preeminent movement designed to place publishing in Afro-American hands—the Black Aesthetic. This creative and critical movement enjoined: "Build Black Institutions!"

I embraced the injunction with passion. My essays on Toomer, Countee Cullen, and Amiri Baraka all appeared under the aegis of institutions that served beneficial ends in their era. Nonetheless, the resources and distributive potential of a series such as the Broadside Critics Series, which first issued my work on Cullen, or a journal like the defunct *Minority Voices,* where my Baraka essay initially appeared, were sharply limited. When the institutions folded, my critical works became difficult or impossible to procure. A reason for reprinting some of the essays included in the present book is to make them easily accessible.

Beyond the matter of access, however, exists the matter of necessary revisions. Candidly, I admit that Cullen deserves a fuller interpretation than I was able to provide in 1973. Similarly, Toomer's *Cane* demands a fuller account than my "New Critical" interpretation of 1972. My revisionary relationship to such authors and essays is made clearer by my autobiographical headnotes. The job of actual revision takes place, primarily, in the new essay constituted by Chapter 3, in this present introduction, and in my concluding remarks.

The critical project represented by the following pages is multifaceted. Perhaps the academic who spoke of grandeur was merely suggesting that essay collections are always the product of *messieurs* who have grand or overly ambitious ideas. I believe, however, that revisionary projects can accomplish significant ends.

Successive drafts on the reservoir of spirit work such as William Wells Brown's continuously revised narrative, Frederick Douglass's autobiographies, Washington's serial compilation of his life story, DuBois' collection of essays in definition of the souls of black folk, Locke's revised collection constituting *The New Negro,* James Baldwin's brilliant autobiographical essays, and Maya Angelou's successive installments on a fascinating life suggest the multiform, ceaseless, and revisionary type of writing that, I hope, characterizes my own project. The most gratifying response that I could receive would be a community's acknowledgment that a black collective enterprise has been moved a bit farther down the road by the following visions and revisions. Such an acknowledgment needn't be grand. A simple "It's like that!" would be grandly sufficient.

I

Journey toward Black Art: Jean Toomer's *Cane*

When I began teaching at Yale in 1968, my ambition was to be a successful critic of British Victorian literature. Having studied at UCLA and the University of Edinburgh, I had produced a dissertation entitled "The Idea in Aestheticism." Commencing with a reading of Dante Gabriel Rossetti, the dissertation argued that nineteenth-century aestheticism ("art for art's sake") was a form of social activism. At a moment when the Vietnam War was in full swing and when America's "flower children" had taken to the streets — often wearing Pre-Raphaelite hairstyles and fashions — in antiwar and anti-establishment protest, the "idea" in the writings of the aesthetes and decadents of nineteenth-century England seemed amenable to interpretation as protest against the vulgar jingoism and ugly industrialization of the Victorian era.

My method of analysis was New Criticism. My education as a scholar of literature had been marked by such criticism, and in 1968 I sincerely believed that "close reading" was an objective mode for wrestling inherent truths from protean works of art. Such truths I deemed unadulterated; they were *artistic,* unbuttressed by historical, sociological, ideological, psychological, or biographical supports. Guided by this New Critical perspective, I was holding forth one evening in New Haven on the virtues of a modern play which was in performance by the Yale Repertory Company. A group of young black men and women broke my concentration when they entered the auditorium. But they seemed to tune in immediately to what I was saying. Their stares were intense and unyielding. When I concluded my talk, the group approached and their leader said: "Brother, did anyone ever tell you how much you look like Malcolm X?" I hardly knew what to say.

The group, as it turned out, was composed of graduate students in Yale's Drama School. They were trying to secure a black drama workshop within the school, and they had also organized themselves to protest some inanely racist play scheduled for production by the repertory company. They were all engaged in creative and political activities in the black New Haven community. They were black nationalists in politics and cultural orientation, whose motto was: "The ultimate solution is Black Revolution!" Saluting my "way with words," they enlisted me in their struggle.

As my hair exploded beyond normal limits, so, too, did my intellectual horizons. Granted permission to teach a black American literature course during 1969–70, I also had the good fortune to secure a contract from McGraw-Hill for an anthology of black American literature. My response to my reading and study of black literature and culture was analogous to Frederick Douglass's response when his master unwittingly informed him of the virtues of literacy:

> I now understood what had been to me a most perplexing difficulty — to wit, the white man's power to enslave the black man. It was a grand achievement, and I prized it highly. From that moment, I understood the pathway from slavery to freedom. . . . Though conscious of the difficulty of learning without a teacher, I set out with high hope, and a fixed purpose, at whatever cost of trouble, to learn how to read.

I set out to learn how to read black American literature.

While my habits of New Critical explication offered an available avenue, I realized from conversations with my Drama School friends that no merely *formal* approach devoid of social, historical, and biographical considerations would suffice for the job of reading black literature. In fact, the elegant black novelist, poet, and critic Arna Bontemps — who joined the Yale English department faculty in 1969—explained to me that his own generation understood that the very orientation of New Criticism consciously excluded expressive traditions grounded in folklore, history, and psychobiography. The utterances of a new generation of black writers that included Amiri Baraka, Larry Neal, and Addison Gayle, Jr., were declarations of war against such exclusion. Clearly, a crisis of allegiance was at hand for me.

The hundreds of black American expressive works that I eagerly, profitably, and enjoyably devoured during 1969–70 were far too compelling to permit me simply to withdraw. I knew that I had to harmonize with the Black Aesthetic temper of a new era. And that meant I would have to adopt an avowedly sociohistorical, biographical, and consciously ideological approach to criticism, reading black texts as works produced by "interested" black men and women. Further, it meant that I would, per force, have to ascribe comprehensible social purpose to all works of expressive culture. *Art,* thus, came to be defined as precisely *not* for art's sake.

Along with other Black Aestheticians, I came to regard art as both a product and a producer in an unceasing struggle for black liberation. To be "art," the product had to be expressivity or performance designed to free minds and bodies of a subjugated people.

Which is to say, we of the Black Aesthetic temper rewrote "art" to mirror the role we had set for ourselves. Deeming ourselves members of a Black Power or Black Liberation cadre, we believed we could be articulate spokespeople to and for the masses. Our aim was to emulate the expressive cultural work of, say, David Walker, Frederick Douglass, Frances Harper, W. E. B. DuBois, or Langston Hughes before us. We read a definite and deliberate social purpose in the efforts of our predecessors, men and women like Sojourner Truth who had so ably moved mass black audiences. We also credited our precursors with a rather more elusive quality called "soul." "Soul" was the most ubiquitous term of the Black Aesthetic era. "Blackness" and "soul" came to compete, in fact, as signs for an ineffable "something" that made black American creativity *Not-Art.*

This brief account indicates that there was a sometimes confusing array of claims and strategies surrounding the Black Aesthetic. The critical framework that it sanctioned, however, was a pure product of an era in which competing claims abounded: Civil Rights vs. Black Power, Black Capitalism vs. Black Utopianism, Black Studies vs. a "Black University," "Negro" vs. "Black," American Reform vs. Black Revolution. In harmony with the competing ideologies and ambivalent orientations of its era, the Black Aesthetic represented a politically interested demand for "engaged" literature. It was also a clarion call for a firmly sociohistorical criticism.

I embraced this aesthetic and all of its claims with belief, joy, and trust. Having grown up in a racist, stultifying Louisville, Kentucky—which, on any given day, could make 1987 Cumming, Georgia, look like Club Med—I had been discriminated against and called "Nigger" enough to think that what America needed was a good Black Revolution. And with the abundant energy and endless enthusiasm of youth, I wanted to speed the day of the revolt. My chosen vocation and recently shifted allegiances, I felt, eminently qualified me as a Black Aesthetician. The rub was that I could not seem to "get it right."

I was never able to speak exactingly or write simply enough to gain the attention of the multiplied thousands of black people—lay people, artists, and critics alike—who so fervently responded to, say, Addison Gayle or Stephen Henderson. There were, at least, two reasons for my shortcomings.

First, I did not know a fraction as much about Afro-American expressivity as Gayle or Henderson. Second, I had not even begun seriously to assess and address the theoretical and practical contradictions implicit in the high value I placed on my "Yale status." My orientation toward Victorian studies was, of course, an emblem of my axiology. For what I relished about the aesthetes and decadents, and the spokesmen who were sources and influences for them, was their "disinterestedness." They refused to be strident ideologues. And their resolute insistence on the saving grace of the contemplative life made them models of quiet revolt. If this sounds like the code of a bourgeois intellectual, then I have successfully described my "Yale status."

Confronted with a conflict between my emotional commitment

to a stridently ideological aesthetic and my intellectual affinity for a disinterested reading of life, I was always writing with two audiences peering over my shoulder—Addison Gayle and Matthew Arnold. The response that "Journey toward Black Art: Jean Toomer's *Cane*" first received mirrors my conflict. Both *PMLA* and the Broadside Critics Series politely rejected the work. *PMLA* said the essay offered "nothing new" on the subject. Broadside said it was too academic.

What was my ambition in writing the essay? I wanted, first, to praise *Cane* as an exception to what was commonly labeled the exotic fare of the Harlem Renaissance. Second, I wanted to put Toomer's work forward as an example of the way in which "our" black literature transcended American minstrel limitations. The book's stream-of-consciousness narration and laconic imagery made it "modern" by white standards.

But outside my confused chauvinism (e.g., proving *Cane* great by white standards), there was the question of actual, practical critical procedures. How could I best show Toomer's work to advantage? The answer, implicit in the analysis that follows, was New Criticism. There was also the question of *Cane*'s status vis-à-vis the criterion of "soul." Was the book black or soulful enough to merit analysis? It was de rigueur for me to believe that *Cane* had a discoverable black, and liberating, *telos*.

My critical posture, as represented by "Journey toward Black Art," suggests, of course, that I was between two equally questionable intellectual positions. While an awareness of what might be called the *cultural situatedness* of *Cane* is surely necessary for any comprehensive critical analysis of Toomer's work, this awareness can be achieved only by meditation, study, and a great deal of reading. It cannot simply be ascribed as an affective function of ideological enthusiasm. Again, while attentive or close reading is needed to apprehend the force of *Cane,* such reading cannot assume, in advance of the evidence, that its result will be a holistic, organic, *literary* masterpiece. Such an assumption is a self-fulfilling prophecy.

The paradox of my situation lay in the fact that I was intent on producing a black art and criticism. My "objective" standards and procedures were, however, discoverably white. "Journey toward Black Art" is, thus, a reflexive enterprise, using a claimed "progress" of both Toomer and his narrator as an emblem of the possibility of transcending the limitations of a black past (a "false" or "failed" Harlem Renaissance). The essay also reads *Cane* as an augury of the emergence of an authentic black art wrung from a fabric of painful contradictions.

In some ways I suspect the essay is more characteristic of the Black Aesthetic in general than even its senior mentors could have recognized when it appeared in my book *Singers of Daybreak* (1974). The essay is governed by a well-intentioned, culturally nationalist, and, I would argue, much-needed black American political perspective. But it is also moved by traditional New Critical means of analysis. It offers a view of the Black Aesthetic critical situation similar to that of Langston Hughes's Leontyne in the poet's twelve moods for jazz:

> In the pot behind the
> Paper doors what's cooking?
> What's smelling, Leontyne?
> Lieder, lovely Lieder
> And a leaf of collard green,
> Lovely Lieder Leontyne.

Traditional "art" songs and odiferous Afro-American critical intentions marked both the Black Aesthetic and the "Journey toward Black Art" that was produced behind its paper doors.

William Stanley Braithwaite's "The Negro in American Literature" concludes with the rhapsodic assertion that "*Cane* is a book of gold and bronze, of dusk and flame, of ecstasy and pain, and Jean Toomer is a bright morning star of a new day of the race in literature."[1] Written in 1924, Braithwaite's statement reflects the energy and excess, the vibrancy and hope of a generation of young black authors who set out in the 1920s to express their "individual dark-skinned selves without fear or shame."[2] They were wooed by white patrons; they had their work modified beyond recognition by theatrical producers, and they were told time and again precisely what type of black American writing the public would accept. Some, like Wallace Thurman, could not endure the strain.[3] Claude McKay absented himself from Harlem throughout most of the twenties,[4] and Langston Hughes and Countee Cullen gained a degree of notoriety.[5] Ironically, it was *Cane* (1923), a book written by a very light complexioned mulatto, that both portrayed — without fear or shame — a dark-skinned self that transcended the concerns of a single period and also heralded much of value that has followed its publication. Arna Bontemps writes:

> Only two small printings were issued, and these vanished quickly. However, among the most affected was practically an entire generation of young Negro writers then just beginning to emerge; their reaction to Toomer's *Cane* marked an awakening that soon thereafter began to be called a Negro Renaissance.[6]

The 1920s presented a problem for the writer who wished to give a full and honest representation of black American life; for him the traditional images, drawn from the authors of the Plantation Tradition and the works of Paul Laurence Dunbar, were passé. The contemporary images, captured in Carl Van Vechten's *Nigger Heaven* (1926) and Claude McKay's *Home to Harlem* (1928), were not designed to elucidate a complex human existence, for they were reflections of that search for the bizarre and the exotic that was destined to flourish in an age of raccoon coats, bathtub gin, and "wine-flushed, bold-eyed" whites who caught the A-train to Harlem and spent an evening slumming, or seeking some élan vital for a decadent but prosperous age. That only two small printings of *Cane* appeared during the 1920s is not striking: the miracle is that it was published at all. Toomer did not choose the approbation that a scintillating (if untrue) portrayal of the black man could bring in the twenties, nor did he speak sotto voce about the amazing progress the black man had made in American society and his imminent acceptance by a fond white world. *Cane* is a symbolically complex work that employs lyrical intensity and stream-of-consciousness narration to portray the journey of an artistic soul toward creative fulfillment; it is unsparing in its criticism of the inimical aspects of the black American heritage and resonant in its praise of the spiritual beauty to be discovered there. An examination of the journey toward genuine, liberating black art presented in *Cane* reveals Toomer as a writer of genius and the book itself as a protest novel, a portrait of the artist, and a thorough delineation of the black situation. These aspects of the work explain its signal place among the achievements of the

Jean Toomer

Harlem Renaissance, and they help to clarify the reaction of a white reading public — a public nurtured on the minstrel tradition, the tracts of the New Negro, and the sensational antics of Carl Van Vechten's blacks — which allowed it to go out of print without a fair hearing.

The first section of *Cane* opens with evocative description and a lyrical question. The subject is Karintha, whose:

> skin is like dusk on the eastern horizon,
> O cant you see it, O cant you see it,
> Her skin is like dusk on the eastern horizon
> . . . When the sun goes down.[7]

The repetition and the simile bringing together the human and the nonhuman leave a memorable impression. The reader is directly asked to respond, as were the hearers of such spirituals as "I've Got a Home in Dat Rock" and "Rich man Dives he lived so well / Don't you see?" From the outset, the atmosphere is one of participation, as the reader is invited to contemplate a woman who carries "beauty, perfect as dusk when the sun goes down."

"Karintha," however, offers more than rhapsodic description and contemplation. It is a concise, suggestive sketch of the maturation of a southern woman: from sensuous childhood through promiscuous adolescence to wanton adulthood. The quatrain that serves as the epigraph is repeated twice and acts as a sharp counterpoint to Karintha's life, which is anything but beautiful: "She stoned the cows, and beat her dog, and fought the other children . . ." In a sense, "Karintha" is a prose "The Four Stages of Cruelty," and its exquisite style forces some of its more telling revelations into a type of Hogarthian background, where they are lost to the casual observer.

There are elements of the humorous black preacher tale in the narrator's comment that "even the preacher, who caught her at mischief, told himself that she was as innocently lovely as a November cotton flower," and grim paradox appears after Karintha has given birth to her illegitimate child near the smoldering sawdust pile of the mill:

Weeks after Karintha returned home the smoke was so heavy you
tasted it in water. Someone made a song:

Smoke is on the hills. Rise up.
Smoke is on the hills, O rise
And take my soul to Jesus.

The holy song that accompanies an unholy event is no less
incongruous than the pilgrimages and the fierce, materialistic
rituals in which men engage to gain access to Karintha. For the
heroine is not an enshrined beauty but a victim of the South, where
"homes . . . are most often built on the two room plan. In one,
you cook and eat, in the other you sleep, and there love goes on."
Karintha has been exposed to an adult world too soon, and the
narrator drives home the irony that results when biblical dictates
are juxtaposed with a bleak reality: "Karintha had seen or heard,
perhaps she had felt her parents loving. One could but imitate
one's parents, for to follow them was the way of God." While
some men "do not know that the soul of her was a growing thing
ripened too soon," the narrator is aware that Karintha has been
subjected to conditions that Christianity is powerless to meliorate.
Her life has been corrupted, and the mystery is that her beauty
remains.

The type of duality instanced by Karintha's sordid life and
striking appearance recurs in part 1 and lends psychological point
to the section.[8] The essential theme of "Karintha" is the debase-
ment of innocence. Men are attracted to the heroine but fail to
appreciate what is of value—the spirituality inherent in her dusky
beauty. They are awed by the pure yet wish to destroy it; evil
becomes their good, and they think only in terms of progressive
time and capitalistic abundance—"The young fellows counted the
time to pass before she would be old enough to mate with them"
and ran stills to make her money. These conditions result, in part,
from a southern Manichaeanism; for the land whose heritage
appears in "Karintha" stated its superiority and condoned an in-
humane slavery, spoke of its aristocracy and traded in human
flesh, lauded its natural resources and wantonly destroyed them
to acquire wealth. Good and evil waged an equal contest in a South
that contained its own natural harmonies but considered blacks as

chattels personal, having no rights that a white man need respect. In such an instance, love could only be an anomaly, and the narrator of part 1 seems fully aware of this. When black women are considered property (the materialism surrounding Karintha and Fern) and white women goddesses (the recrimination that accompanies Becky's sacrilegious acts), deep relationships are impossible; the evil of the encompassing universe and the natural compulsion of man to corrupt the beautiful inform the frustrating encounters of part 1.

The two poems—"Reapers" and "November Cotton Flower"—that follow "Karintha" offer a further treatment of the significant themes found in the story. The expectations raised by the title of the first poem are almost totally defeated by its text. There are sharpened blades, black men, black horses, and an inexorable energy; but wearying customs, indifference, and death are also present. "I see them place the hones / In their hip-pockets as a thing that's done," the speaker says, and goes on to depict the macabre death of a field rat that, "startled, squealing bleeds." This event does not halt the movement of the cutters, however: "I see the blade, / Blood-stained, continue cutting . . ." An abundant harvest is not the result of the poem's action, and the black reapers, with scythes in hand, take on the appearance of medieval icons of death—an appropriate image for those who help to corrupt the life of Karintha. "November Cotton Flower" with its images of scarcity, drought, dead birds, and boll weevils continues the portrayal of a grim environment. Against this background, however, stands a beauty like Karintha's. The heroine of the first sketch was compared to a November cotton flower, and here the appearance of the "innocently lovely" flower brings about the speculation of the superstitious. "Beauty so sudden for that time of year," one suspects, is destined to attract its exploiters.

While exploring the nature of Karintha's existence, the author has been constructing the setting that is to appear throughout part 1. The first story's effect is heightened by the presence of the religious, the suggestive, and the feminine, and certain aspects of the landscape linger in the reader's mind: a sawmill, pine trees, red dust, a pyramidal sawdust pile, and rusty cotton stalks. The folk songs convey a feeling of cultural homogeneity; they are all of a religious character, rising spontaneously and pervading the landscape. The finishing details of this setting — the Dixie Pike and the railroad — are added in "Becky," which deals with a mode of interaction characteristic of primitive, homogeneous societies.

"Becky" is the story of a white woman who gives birth to two mulatto sons, thus violating one of the most rigid taboos of southern society. As a consequence, she is ostracized by the community. William Goede (following the lead of Robert Bone) describes her plight as follows:

> Becky is, like Hester Prynne, made to pay for the collective sense of guilt of the community: after whites and Negroes exile her, they secretly build her a house which both sustains and finally buries her. The house, on the other hand, built between the road and the railroad, confines the girl until the day when the roof falls through and kills her.[9]

Unlike Karintha, Becky is seldom portrayed in physical terms. The narrator has never seen her, and the community as a whole merely speculates on her actions and her changing appearance. She is primarily a psychological presence to whom the community pays an ironical homage: a spectral representation of the southern miscegenatory impulse that was so alive during the days of American slavery and was responsible for countless lynchings even in Toomer's own day. As early as the seventeenth century, southern legislatures were enacting laws to prevent sexual alliances between blacks and whites; hence, the community in "Becky" reacts in a manner sanctioned by law and custom.

"Becky" presents a further exploration of the duality theme encountered in "Karintha," and here the psychological element seems to predominate. The heroine's exile first calls to mind repression; she is set apart and finally buried. A more accurate description of Becky, however, is that she is a shaman. Among certain Asian groups and American Indian tribes, a person who engages in unsanctioned behavior (homosexuality, for example) is thought to have received a divine summons; he becomes a public figure and devises and leads ritualistic ceremonies that project his abnormal behavior. The function of the shaman is twofold; he enables the community to act out, by proxy, its latent abnormalities, and he reinforces its capacity to resist such tendencies. He is tolerated and revered because of his supernatural power, yet hated as a symbol of moral culpability and as a demanding priest who exacts a penitential toll. The most significant trait of the shaman, however, is that—despite his ascribed powers—he is unable to effect a genuine cure. Georges Devereux explains this paradox:

> Aussi ne peut-on considérer que le chaman accomplit une "cure psychiatrique" au sens *strict* du terme; il procure seulement au malade ce que L'École de psychoanalyse de Chicago appelle une "expérience affective corrective" qui l'aide à réorganiser son système de défense mais ne lui permet pas d'attendre à cette réelle prise de conscience de soi-même (*insight*) sans laquelle il n'y a pas de véritable guérison.[10]

It is not surprising that analysts consider the shaman a disturbed individual; he is often characterized by hysteria and suicidal tendencies, and he remains in his role because he finds relief from his own disorders by granting a series of culturally sanctioned defenses to his followers.

Becky has engaged in a pattern of behavior that the surrounding community considers taboo, and she is relegated to a physical position outside the group but essentially public. Her house is built (by the townspeople) in a highly visible location, an "eye-shaped piece of sandy ground. . . . Islandized between the road and railroad track." The citizens scorn her and consider her deranged ("poor-white crazy woman, said the black folks' mouths"), but at the same time they pray for her, bring her food, and keep her alive. Becky, in turn, continues her activities; she has another mulatto son and remains in the tottering house until it eventually crumbles beneath the weight of its chimney. In essence, we witness the same dichotomy presented in "Karintha"; the South professes racial purity and abhorrence of miscegenation, but the fundamental conditions of the region nourish a subconscious desire for interracial relationships and make a penitential ritual necessary. It seems significant, moreover, that Becky—who is a Catholic and in that respect also one of the South's traditional aversions—assumes a divine role for the community. Attraction toward and repulsion by the spiritually ordained are as much a part of the landscape in "Becky" as in "Karintha."

The narrator is swayed by the attitudes of the townspeople, but he is by no means a devout shamanist. He duly records the fact that Becky's house was built on "sandy ground" (reflecting the destructive and aggressive feelings that are part of the shamanic experience), and he points out that Becky is a Catholic. Moreover, he sets up a contrapuntal rhythm between the natural pines that "whisper to Jesus" and the ambivalent charity of the community. The most devastating note in this orchestration is that Sunday is the day of Becky's destruction, and the vagrant preacher Barlo is unwilling to do more than toss a Bible on the debris that entraps her. In short, the narrator captures the irony inherent in the miscegenatory underconsciousness of the South. The town's experience with Becky provides a "corrective, affective experience" but not a substantive cure; as the story closes (on notes that remind one of the eerie conjure stories of black folklore), one suspects that the townspeople are no more insightful.

At this point, Toomer has set forth the dominant tone, setting, characters, and point of view of the first section. Women are in the forefront, and in both "Karintha" and "Becky" they assume symbolic roles that help to illustrate the dualities of a southern heritage. The beauty of Karintha and the beneficent aspects of Becky's existence are positive counterpoints to the aggressiveness, materialism, and moral obtuseness of the community as a whole. The omnipresent folk songs and the refrain in the second story ("The pines whisper to Jesus") bespeak a commitment to spirituality and beauty, while the animosity of the townspeople in "Becky" and the ineffectiveness of Christianity in "Karintha" display the grimmer side of a lyrically described landscape whose details pervade the whole of *Cane*. The point of view is largely that of a sensitive narrator, whom Arna Bontemps describes:

> Drugged by beauty "perfect as dusk when the sun goes down," lifted and swayed by folk song, arrested by eyes that "desired nothing that *you* could give," silenced by "corn leaves swaying, rusty with talk," he recognized that "the Dixie Pike has grown from a goat path in Africa." A native richness is here, he concluded, and the poet embraced it with the passion of love.[11]

The narrator speaks in a tone that combines awe and reverence with effective irony and subtle criticism. There are always deeper levels of meaning beneath his highly descriptive surface, and this is not surprising when one considers Toomer's statement that in the South "one finds soil in the sense that the Russians know it — the soil every art and literature that is to live must be embedded in."[12]

The emblematic nature of the soil is reflected in the tone and technique of the narrator and particularly in the book's title. Throughout part 1 there is an evocation of a land of sugarcane whose ecstasy and pain are rooted in a communal soil. But the title conveys more than this. Justifications of slavery on scriptural grounds frequently traced the black man's ancestry to the race of Cain, the slayer of Abel, in the book of Genesis. Toomer is concerned not only with the southern soil but also with the sons of Cain who populate it. In a colloquial sense, "to raise Cain" is to create disorder and cacophony, and in a strictly denotative sense, a cane is an instrument of support. Toomer's narrator is attempting to create an ordered framework that will contain the black American's complex existence, offer supportive values, and act as a guide for the perceptive soul's journey from amorphous experience to a finished work of art.

The third story of part 1, "Carma," is called by the narrator "the crudest melodrama," and so it is — on one level. When Carma's husband, Bane (surely an ironical name to set against *karma*), discovers that she has been unfaithful, he slashes the man who has told him, and is sentenced to the chain gang. This is melodramatic to be sure, but only (to quote the narrator) "as I have told it." Beneath the sensational surface is a tragedy of black American life. Bane, like Jimboy in Langston Hughes's *Not without Laughter,* is forced by economic pressures to seek work away from home; thus, his wife is left alone in an environment where (again, according to the narrator) promiscuity is a norm.[13] But Carma is also a woman who flaunts her sensuality, and can hardly be said to possess a strong sense of responsibility.

As in the previous stories, there are positive and redeeming elements in "Carma." The heroine herself is "strong as any man," and, given her name, this at least implies that her spirituality — that which is best and most ineffable in her — is capable of enduring the

inimical aspects of her surroundings. This is particularly important
when one considers that "Carma" introduces a legendary African
background to the first section: "Torches flare . . . juju men, gree-
gree, witch-doctors . . . torches go out. . . . The Dixie Pike has
grown from a goat path in Africa" (pp. 17–18). The passage that
introduces this reflection reads: "From far away, a sad strong song.
Pungent and composite, the smell of farmyards is the fragrance
of the woman. She does not sing; her body is a song. She is in
the forest, dancing" (p. 17). The folk song is linked to the African
past, and a feeling of cultural continuity is established. The
atavistic remains of a ceremonial past have the fragrance of earth
and the spirituality of song and dance to recommend them, and
at the center of this drama is Carma. She is strong (as Karintha
is beautiful) despite southern conditions, and she endures in the
face of an insensitive Bane, who is enraged because he cannot
master his destiny.

"Carma" is also the first story in which the narrator clearly identifies himself as a conscious recounter ("whose tale as I have told
it"), and the poems that follow read like invocations to the heritage
that he is exploring. "Song of the Son" states his desire to sing
the "souls of slavery," and "Georgia Dusk," which makes further
use of the legendary background encountered in "Carma," evokes
the spirits of the "unknown bards" of the past. It is not surprising, then, that the story of Fern should follow.

Fern is a woman whom men used until they realized there was
nothing they could do for her that would modify her nature or
bring them peace. She is an abandoned Karintha, and in a sense
a more beautiful and alluring Esther (heroine of the next story),
staring at the world with haunting eyes. The narrator seeks out
this beautiful exile who is free in her sexuality and unmoved by the
all-pervasive cash nexus of her environment. However, when he
asks himself the question posed by former suitors—"What could
I do for her?"—his answer is that of the artist: "Talk, of course.
Push back the fringe of pines upon new horizons" (p. 29). The
others answered in solely materialistic terms, coming away from
their relationships with Fern oblivious to her fundamental character and vowing to do greater penitence: "candy every week . . .
a magnificent something with no name on it . . . a house . . .

rescue her from some unworthy fellow who had tricked her into marrying him" (pp. 25–26). The narrator, on the other hand, aspires to project a vision that will release Fern from her stifling existence; she thus becomes for him an inspiration, an artistic ideal. She is a merger of black American physical attractiveness and the unifying myth so important in black American history and in the creation of the spirituals.

"If you have heard a Jewish cantor sing, if he has touched you and made your own sorrow seem trivial when compared with his, you will know my [the narrator's] feeling when I follow the curves of her profile, like mobile rivers, to their common delta," and Fern's full name is Fernie May Rosen. The narrator is thus making use of the seminal comparison between the history of the Israelites and that of black America, which frequently appears in the religious lore of black American culture. In effect, the slaves appropriated the myth of the Egyptian captivity and considered themselves favored by God and destined in time to be liberated by His powers; this provided unity for a people who found themselves uprooted and defined by whites — historians and others — as descendants of wild savages on the "dark continent" of Africa.[14] Despite the fact that she dislikes the petty people of the South and apparently needs to express an underlying spirituality, Fern seems to act as a symbolic representation of the black man's adoption of this myth. When the narrator has brought about a hysterical release in her, however, he fails to comprehend what he has evoked. The story ends with an injunction to the reader to seek out Fern when he travels south. The narrator feels that his ideal holds significance, but claims that his aspirations toward it are unfulfilled. There appears to be some disingenuousness in this claim; for the teller of Fern's story has thoroughly explored the ironies inherent in the merger of white religion and black servitude. The religion of the Israelites is out of place in the life of Fern. While she captures — in her mysterious song like that of a Jewish cantor — the beauty of its spirit (and, in this sense, stands outside the narrow-minded community), she is imprisoned by the mores it occasions. Like Becky and Karintha, Fern is a victim, and the narrator skillfully captures her essence. The apparent disingenuousness at the story's conclusion is in reality modesty; for the art the narrator implies is humble actually holds great significance (in its subtle didactic elements) for the culture he is attempting to delineate.

"Esther" is a story of alienation and introduces an element of inquietude that grows into the concluding terror of the book's first section. Apocalyptic images abound as the heroine dreams of King Barlo (a figure who first appeared in "Becky") overcoming her pale frigidity with a flaming passion that will result in a "black, singed, woolly, tobacco-juice baby — ugly as sin" (p. 41). Edward Waldron points out that

> beneath this superficial level . . . lie at least two more intense and, for Toomer, more personal interpretations. One deals with the relationship of a light-skinned American Negro to the black community in which he (she) must try to function, and the other has to do with a common theme of the Harlem Renaissance, the relationship between the American Negro and Africa.[15]

But one can make excessive claims for King Barlo. While it is true that he falls into a religious trance and sketches, in symbolic oratory, the fate of Africans at the hands of slave traders, it is also true that he is a vagrant preacher, a figure whom Toomer sketches fully (and with less than enthusiasm) in Layman of "Kabnis." And though Barlo is the prophet of a new dawn for the black American, he is also a businessman[16] who makes money during the war, and a lecherous frequenter of the demimonde. It thus seems an overstatement to make a one-to-one correlation between Barlo and Africa, or Afro-America. It is necessary to bear in mind that Esther Crane is not only a "tragic mulatto" repressed by Protestant religion and her father's business ethic ("Esther sells lard and snuff and flour to vague black faces that drift in her store to ask for them"), she is a fantasizer as well. Esther's view of Barlo is the one presented to the reader through most of the story; hence, when she retreats fully from reality at the conclusion, the reader's judgments should be qualified accordingly.

Esther's final state is described as follows: "She draws away, frozen. Like a somnambulist she wheels around and walks stiffly to the stairs. Down them. . . . She steps out. There is no air, no street, and the town has completely disappeared" (p. 48). The heroine is enclosed in her own mind; the sentient objects of the world mean nothing to this repressed sleepwalker. Given the complexity of Barlo's character, it is impossible to feel that such an observer could capture it accurately. Just as we refuse to accept the middle-aged and sentimental reflections of Marlowe as the final analysis of Kurtz in Conrad's "Heart of Darkness" and exercise a qualifying restraint before the words of Camus's narrator in *The Fall*, so we must recognize the full nature of Esther's character if we are to grasp her story and the role of King Barlo in it. Barlo does contain within himself the unifying myth of black American culture, and he delivers it to the community in the manner of the most accomplished black folk preachers. In this character, however, he paradoxically contributes to Esther's stifled sensibility, which continually projects visions of sin. As a feat hero (the best cotton picker) and a skillful craftsman of words (his moving performance on the public street), he contains positive aspects, but the impression that remains—when one has noted his terrified and hypocritical response in "Becky" and his conspicuous materialism and insensitive treatment of Esther—is not as favorable as some critics would tempt us to believe.[17]

The feelings of alienation and foreshadowing generated by "Esther" are heightened by the poems that follow. "Conversion" tells of a degraded "African Guardian of Souls" who has drunkenly embraced white religiosity, and seems intended further to illuminate the character of Barlo. "Portrait in Georgia" is a subtle, lyrical protest poem in which a woman is described in terms of the instruments and actions of a lynching. The second poem's vision prefigures the horror of the last story in part 1, "Blood-Burning Moon."

"Blood-Burning Moon" stands well in the company of such Harlem Renaissance works as Claude McKay's "If We Must Die" and Walter White's *The Fire in the Flint*. It is a work that protests, in unequivocal terms, the senseless, brutal, and sadistic violence perpetrated against the black man by white America. The narrator realized in "Carma" that violence was a part of southern existence, and the shattering demise of Becky, Barlo's religious trance, and Fern's frantic outpouring speak volumes about the terror of such a life. But in "Blood-Burning Moon" the narrator traces southern violence to its source. Tom Burwell—strong, dangerous, black lover of Louisa and second to Barlo in physical prowess—is only one of the black Americans whom the Stone family "practically owns." Louisa—black and alluring—works for the family, and Bob Stone (who during the days of slavery would have been called "the young massa") is having an affair with her. Tom reacts to hints and rumors of this affair in the manner of Bane; he turns violently on the gossipers and refuses to acknowledge what he feels to be true. Wage slavery, illicit alliances across the color line, intraracial violence—the narrator indeed captures the soul of America's "peculiar institution," and the results are inevitable. In a confrontation between Stone and Burwell, the black man's strength triumphs, and the white mob arrives (in "high-powered cars with glaring search-lights" that remind one of the "ghost train" in "Becky") to begin its gruesome work. The lynching of Tom, which drives Louisa insane, more than justifies the story's title. The moon, controller of tides and destinies, and a female symbol, brings blood and fire to the black American.

Part 1 is a combination of awe-inspiring physical beauty, human hypocrisy, restrictive religious codes, and psychological trauma. In "Fern" the narrator says: "That the sexes were made to mate is the practice of the South" (p. 26). But sexual consummation in the first section often results in dissatisfaction or in a type of perverse motherhood. Men come away from Fern frustrated; Karintha covertly gives birth to her illegitimate child in a pine forest; Esther dreams of the immaculate conception of a tobacco-stained baby; and Becky's sons are illegitimate mulattoes, who first bring violence to the community and then depart from it with curses. The women of part 1 are symbolic figures, but the lyrical terms in which they are described can be misleading. With the exception of their misdirected sexuality, they are little different from the entrapped and stifled women of the city seen in part 2. In short, something greater than the pressure of urban life accounts for the black man's frustrated ambitions, violent outbursts, and tragic deaths at the hands of white America. The black American's failure to fully comprehend the beautiful in his own heritage—the Georgia landscape, folk songs, and women of deep loveliness—is part of it. But the narrator places even greater emphasis on the black man's ironical acceptance of the "strange cassava" and "weak palabra" of a white religion. Throughout part 1, he directs pointed thrusts—in the best tradition of David Walker, Frederick Douglass, and William Wells Brown[18]—at Christianity. Although he appreciates the rich beauty of black folk songs that employ Protestant religious imagery ("Georgia Dusk"), he also sees that the religion as it is practiced in the South is often hypocritical and stifling. The narrator, as instanced by "Nullo," the refrain in "Becky," and a number of fine descriptive passages throughout the first section, seems to feel a deeper spirituality in the landscape. Moreover, there seems more significance in the beauty of Karintha or in the eyes of Fern (into which flow "the countryside and something that I call God") than in all the cramped philanthropy, shouted hosannas, vagrant preachers, and religious taboos of Georgia. The narrator, in other words, clearly realizes that the psychological mimicry that led to the adoption of a white religion often directed black Americans away from their own spiritual beauties and resulted in destruction.[19]

But the importance of white America's role cannot be minimized. King Barlo views the prime movers behind the black situation as "little white-ant biddies" who tied the feet of the African, uprooted him from his traditional culture, and made him prey to alien gods. The essential Manichaeanism of a South that thrived on slavery, segregation, the chattel principle, and violence is consummately displayed in the first section of *Cane,* and Barlo realizes that a new day must come before the black man will be free. The brutality directed against the black American has slowed the approach of such a dawn, but the narrator of part 1 has discovered positive elements in the black southern heritage that may lead to a new day: a sense of song and soil, and the spirit of a people who have their severe limitations but cannot be denied.

Part 2 of *Cane* is set in the city and constitutes a male cycle. The creative soul that was characterized by a type of "negative capability" in part 1 becomes an active agency of dreams and knowledge, and the narrator recedes to a more objective plane, where he can view even himself somewhat impartially. "Avey" has a first-person point of view, but the remainder of the stories come from the hand of an omniscient narrator who seems aware that as a creator he needs "consummate skill to walk upon the waters where huge bubbles burst" (p. 108). The urban environment demands more careful analysis, and thus the lyrical impulse is diminished in the second section—there are only half as many connecting poems here as in part 1.

"Seventh Street" and "Rhobert," the opening sketches of part 2, capture the positive and negative aspects of a new environment. The driving, cutting, inexorable energy seen in "Reapers" and "Cotton Song" has become "A crude-boned, soft-skinned wedge of nigger life" thrusting its way "into the white and white-washed wood of Washington" (p. 71). And the epigraph of the first sketch evokes a lower-echelon black urban environment—with its easy spending, bootleggers, silken shirts, and Cadillacs—not a dusky, natural beauty like Karintha's. The setting, however, is not a bizarre and exotic world; it is a life fathered by the incongruous combination of senseless violence ("the war") and puritan morality ("Prohibition"). Unlike the southern environment with its African ancestry, Seventh Street is a disharmony of nature—"a bastard"—and its rhythms reflect its cacophonous birth: thrusting, jazzy, crude-boned. These rhythms cannot be absorbed by the white world that surrounds them: "Stale soggy wood of Washington. Wedges rust in soggy wood . . . Split it! In two! Again! Shred it! . . . the sun. Wedges are brilliant in sun; ribbons of wet wood dry and blow away" (p. 71). The new life is an agency of the sun rather than the moon, and those who set it to work can neither contain nor arrest it. This situation becomes sardonically humorous when the narrator comments: "God would not dare to suck black red blood. A Nigger God! He would duck his head in shame and call for the Judgment Day." The omnipotent Father (frequently pictured by church primers as a blue-eyed white man) would be irrevocably altered by one drop of black blood. But there are black Americans who fear this new life. They wear their God-built houses like divers' helmets and refuse to subject themselves to its pressures. Rhobert—who might appropriately be called "robot"—is ruled by the white ethical code (the house) that has been imposed upon him.[20] After reading "Rhobert" and "Seventh Street," one is aware that one is in the presence of a narrator who has learned to look intelligently beneath the surface of life. His irony is more subtle, and the near-Swiftian satire of the second sketch demonstrates his ability to make accurate, undisguised value judgments. Moreover, he has moved toward greater self-knowledge; if Rhobert is portrayed as a man engaged in a somewhat fruitless contest, so, too, is the first-person narrator of "Avey."

Goede has pointed out that "Avey," "Box Seat," and "Kabnis" represent portraits of the black American artist,[21] and "Avey's" narrator clearly identifies himself as a writer near the end of the story. Avey, whom Darwin Turner calls "an educated and northern Karintha,"[22] acts as a sensual ideal for the narrator and his boyhood peers; they long to mate with her and seek to give something she desires. Avey, however, is extraordinarily indifferent to them. She pursues an uneventful life and finally becomes a prostitute.

Despite the humor he directs at her indifference ("Hell! she was no better than a cow. I was certain that she was a cow when I felt an udder in a Wisconsin stock-judging class"), Avey becomes an artistic ideal for the narrator. Having seen her, he cannot forget her and longs to do something for her. Unlike the setting of "Fern," the backdrop for the narrator's quest in "Avey" is not in harmony with his designs. V Street in Washington's black community, an amusement park, the Potomac River, Harpers Ferry, and Soldier's Home — the sounds that rise from this landscape are not resonant folk songs: "The engines of this valley have a whistle, the echoes of which sound like iterated gasps and sobs. I always think of them as crude music from the soul of Avey" (p. 81).

At the outset of "Avey," the narrator comments:

> I like to think now that there was a hidden purpose in the way we [he and his childhood friends] hacked them [boxes on V Street containing saplings] with our knives. I like to feel that something deep in me responded to the trees, the young trees that whinnied like colts impatient to be let free. (P. 76)

As the story progresses, the manner in which he hopes to bestow freedom becomes less violent, and in his last encounter with Avey, he (as in "Fern") conceives of talk as artistic expression, as an agency of liberation:

I talked, beautifully I thought, about an art that would be born, an art that would open the way for women the likes of her. I asked her to hope, and build up an inner life against the coming of that day. I recited some of my own things to her. I sang, with a strange quiver in my voice, a promise-song. (P. 87)

But while the narrator evoked, at least, a hysterical response from Fern, he finds Avey asleep when he has finished talking. He realizes finally that Avey's is not the type of loveliness that characterizes a new day: "She did not have the gray crimson-splashed beauty of the dawn."

Bone ventures the idea that "Toomer's intellectualizing males are tragic because they value talking above feeling,"[23] but such a formulation implies that beautiful talk and profound feelings are mutually exclusive in *Cane,* which is not the case. The narrator derides himself for having "dallied dreaming" instead of making advances to Avey during a youthful holiday, and he realizes the absurdity of his situation when he finds her asleep. However, he also depicts himself as a man with his mind "set on freedom" and knows that art can play a role in achieving this end. Moreover, he is the character who evokes that sense of song and soil that received such positive valuations in part 1. He describes the setting for his final meeting with Avey as follows: "And when the wind is from the South, soil of my homeland falls like a fertile shower upon the lean streets of the city." And during the encounter, he reflects: "I wanted the Howard Glee Club to sing 'Deep River, Deep River,' from the road." The glee club's song is proposed as a substitute for the tinny, regimental music of the band, just as the narrator's dreams and visions are posed as liberating forces for the life of Avey. The feeling of frustration that concludes the story, therefore, results not totally from a flaw in the narrator's character but also from the intractability of his artistic materials. Avey, who is one of the more languorous and promiscuous members of the new urban black bourgeoisie, is hopelessly insensible to the artist's rendering of "a larger life," and one would scarcely expect her to respond to a beautiful heritage. She is, indeed, an "orphan-woman."

In the poems "Beehive" and "Storm Ending," the narrator first views the "black hive" as a place where he can rest indifferently,

taking his pleasures in the manner of Avey. He soon realizes, however, that "Earth is a waxen cell of the world comb" and longs to
move outward toward greater fulfillment — "And curl forever in
some far-off farmyard flower." The images of pleasure in "Beehive"
are transmuted to ones of disharmony in "Storm Ending." Honey
becomes rain, and flowers appear as ominous thunder from which
the earth flees. Together, the poems seem to offer a further comment on "Avey." While Avey is alluring and a member of that
class of blacks who (during Toomer's day) sought their alliances
among college-bred men and women, she is unable (or unwilling)
to respond to the beauties of her heritage. She cannot listen with
interest to the narrator's evocations of the past or to his idealistic
projections of a future black American creativity that will release
men from their stifling existence. There is not only insensitivity in
Avey's reaction but also a kind of tragedy, since it makes her an
even greater victim of the urban anonymity and disharmony that
confronted so many blacks after their migration from the South to
the North at the beginning of the twentieth century. Hence, the
transvaluation of images that occurs between "Beehive" and "Storm
Ending" offers another instance of the duality theme; when one has
penetrated the cardboard masks labeled "progress" and "the New
Negro," one is likely to find the same obliviousness to life and to
society's deeper meanings that appears repeatedly in part 1.

With the exception of "Bona and Paul," the stories and poems
that follow "Storm Ending" in part 2 are restatements of concerns
that have been treated earlier. The protagonists of "Theater" and
"Box Seat" are both dreamers who envision passionate affairs with
women bound by convention. Dorris in "Theater," like Muriel
in "Box Seat," dances with energy, but neither could conceive of
saying, in Imamu Baraka's words,

> I want to be sung. I want
> all my bones and meat hummed
> against the thick floating
> winter sky. I want myself
> as dance. As what I am
> given love, or time, or space
> to feel myself.[24]

Dorris uses her dance, which is "of Canebreak loves and man-grove feastings," to solicit from John silk stockings and "kids, and a home, and everything," which she equates with love. And Muriel, after attracting Dan with her dance, is too repressed by societal dictates (represented by "Mrs. Pribby," a name second only to "Mrs. Grundy" in its devastating effects) to accept his love and his vision of life.

Of course, John and Dan have severe shortcomings. John's being, like the speaker's in "Prayer" and the woman's in "Calling Jesus," is fragmented. Dan suffers from a romantic megalomania that leads him to believe he is a type of the new messiah. But while one can imagine either engaging in the stilted, "bower of bliss" romance described in "Her Lips Are Copper Wire" or in the fruit-less self-indulgence of "Harvest Song," both are characters who possess the ability to dream and project rejuvenating images drawn from the black American heritage. John feels himself become the "mass-heart" of the black urban folk (p. 92), and he envisions a Dorris—"Her face is tinted like the autumn alley. Of old flowers, or of a southern canefield, her perfume" (p. 99)—who could share his artistic dreams: "John reaches for a manuscript and reads" (p. 99). In "Box Seat," the narrator's injunction to the "gleaming limbs and asphalt torso" of the street might well have been directed to Dan Moore:

> Shake your curled wool-blossoms, nigger. Open your liver lips to the lean, white spring. Stir the root-life of a withered people. Call them from their houses, and teach them to dream. (P. 104)

The dream is one of the most important elements in the second section; it can reunify the body and the soul separated by northern life ("Calling Jesus"), and it can stir the "root-life" of black Ameri-cans given to the mindless pleasures (the popular theater or Crim-son Gardens) of the city and hemmed in by its rigid structures— moral codes, box seats, houses. The artist may be affected by the malaise of urban life, and as a consequence he may withdraw so far from it that his imaginative vision fragments the self (like John's in "Theater"), obscuring the physical beauty before him (Dorris's dance)—but he is the bringer of dreams.

The whole of part 2 might justifiably be called a portrait of the artist who has been removed from a primitive and participatory culture to suffer the alienation of modern life. One means of overcoming this estrangement is the dream, which calls forth positive images from the past; but when the artist's reveries become — for any reason — simply acts of self-indulgence (a word that might describe John's imaginings), he must move beyond the dream in a search for greater self-knowledge and a broader definition of the artist's role. The theme of "Bona and Paul," the concluding story of the second section, involves such a quest. When the story opens, Paul has become so introspective that his associates are baffled; even Bona, who is white (reviving the miscegenation theme of "Becky" and "Blood-Burning Moon"), though attracted to Paul, fails to comprehend him. Action is limited in the story: four students from a regimented physical education college in Chicago go on a date to Crimson Gardens. The primary focus of the largely stream-of-consciousness narration is the mind of Paul, which "follows the sun to a pine-matted hillock in Georgia" (p. 137). The passage following this description holds significance for "Bona and Paul" and for *Cane* as a whole:

> He sees the slanting roofs of gray unpainted cabins tinted lavender. A Negress chants a lullaby beneath the mate-eyes of a southern planter. Her breasts are ample for the suckling of a song. She weans it, and sends it, curiously weaving, among lush melodies of cane and corn. Paul follows the sun into himself in Chicago. (P. 138)

The essence of the black southern heritage is in Paul's dream, but what is more important is that the dreamer incorporates the sun of this heritage into himself: "He is at Bona's window. With his own eyes he looks through a dark pane." Bona contains no light, and Art, Paul's roommate, "is like the electric light which he snaps on." At Crimson Gardens the illumination is artificial. Paul, whom Bona designates "a poet — or a gym instructor," becomes a source of natural light, and he is neither a lyric poet like the speaker of "Reapers" nor a regimented victim of "mental concepts" like the drillers seen at the beginning of the story. He has transcended a narrowly personal stage of art and moves toward a stance as the knowing, philosophical creator.

His epiphany occurs at Crimson Gardens:

Suddenly he knew that people saw, not attractiveness in his dark
skin, but difference. Their stares, giving him to himself, filled something long empty within him, and were like green blades sprouting
in his consciousness. There was fullness, and strength and peace
about it all. He saw himself, cloudy, but real. (P. 145)

Paul turns first to a brief exploration of the white world, which
he finds lovely in its artificial light. He dances with Bona, and
passion flares for an instant. The couple leaves the garden. But
night is alien to Bona:

Perhaps for some reason, white skins are not supposed to live at
night. Surely, enough nights would transform them fantastically,
or kill them. And their red passion? Night pales that too, and made
it moony. (P. 141)

When Paul is suddenly possessed by the night and the face of
the black doorman (the man outside the garden), Bona realizes
that she cannot contain, or comprehend, his desires. The fact that
Bona has left when Paul returns does not mean the story's conclusion is pessimistic. Paul has come to greater self-knowledge,
and he turns from Bona in an attempt to share it with another
black man. The departure of Bona simply reinforces Paul's initial
assessment:

From the South. What does that mean, precisely, except that you'll
love or hate a nigger? Thats a lot. What does it mean except that
in Chicago you'll have the courage to neither love or hate. A priori.
(P. 148)

It is Bona who is cold, imprisoned by the white mental restraints
her companion has rejected. Paul is like a nascent black sun and
has taken the first step toward sharing his vision with his people.
Part 2, therefore, moves beyond the dream to knowledge:

I'd like to know you whom I look at. Know, not love. Not that
knowing is a greater pleasure; but that I have just found the joy
of it. You came just a month too late. Even this afternoon I
dreamed. (P. 148)

From the lyrical, awed, contemplative narrator of "Karintha,"
Cane has progressed to a self-conscious, philosophical creator who

contains "his own glow" and rejects the artificial garden of white life. "Kabnis," the concluding section of *Cane,* deals with the actions of such an artist vis-à-vis black southern life. It brings the action of the book full circle and completes the portrait of the artist.

The narrator of "Avey" seeks "the simple beauty of another's soul" and "the truth that people bury in their hearts" (pp. 85–86). The artist in "Kabnis," however, searches for knowledge of his own soul and an artistic design that will express it. From the simple observation of the physical beauty of women, the narrator has moved to a fuller exploration of the complexities that beset the black soul. Most of the symbolic figures in the drama are men, and the process of making undisguised value judgments, at work in "Rhobert," is fundamental to "Kabnis." The work is not only a return to the South but also an open protest (as opposed to the subtle, lyrical criticism dominant in part 1) against its stifling morality and brutal violence.

Though a number of recent critics have insisted that Ralph Kabnis is an unsympathetic character,[25] Bontemps correctly states that the protagonist "is a languishing idealist finally redeemed from cynicism and dissipation by the discovery of underlying strength in his people."[26] And Goede is tellingly accurate when he writes:

> In Kabnis Jean Toomer has discovered an appropriate symbol of the Negro writers who hope to stir "the root-life of a withered people." Like [Ralph] Ellison's hero-writer [in *Invisible Man*], Toomer's hero-writer senses at least the first tentative step toward a commitment, through art, to racial experiences of the Negro.[27]

Ralph Kabnis is a Northerner who has come south to teach. He is fired by Hanby, the school superintendent (and an unctuous counterpart to Mrs. Pribby), and taken in by the wagonsmith, Halsey. Kabnis meets Layman, a southern preacher, and Lewis, a Northerner who has made a contract with himself — presumably to investigate the South for a month. The introspective Kabnis proves a hopeless failure as a manual worker and spends much of his time in the cellar of the wagon shop, which is reached by stairs located behind "a junk heap." "Besides being the home of a

very old man, . . . [the cellar] is used by Halsey on those occasions when he spices up the life of the small town." The old man
is attended by Carrie K., Halsey's sister, and when first encountered he has been mumbling and fasting for two weeks. Halsey
arranges a night of debauchery for himself, Kabnis, and Lewis,
and the play concludes on the morning afterward, when the old
man speaks. As in "Bona and Paul," however, action plays a
minor role in "Kabnis"; description, dialogue, and reflection provide the points of focus. The message they render is that the old
ethic of the southern black man — composed of Protestantism,
vocational education, shopkeeping, and accommodation — will not
suffice in a violent white society. Moreover, the new scientific
approach to the complexities of black American life, represented
by Lewis — whom Goede equates (I think correctly) with an intellectual "race man" such as W. E. B. DuBois — is unsatisfactory.
Kabnis delivers the following thrust at the scientific attitude in
general:

> You know, Ralph, old man, it wouldn't surprise me at all to see
> a ghost. People dont think there are such things. They rationalize
> their fear, and call their cowardice science. Fine bunch, they are.
> (P. 165)

Negative images also surround all those activities of the black
American's southern existence which the narrator and the author
consider ineffective or inimical, for example, religion:

> God is a profligate red-nosed man about town. Bastardy; me. A
> bastard son has got a right to curse his maker. (Kabnis, p. 161)

> Above its [the church's] squat tower, a great spiral of buzzards
> reaches far into the heavens. An ironic comment upon the path
> that leads into the Christian land . . . (the author, p. 169)

> This preacher-ridden race. Pray and shout. Theyre in the preacher's
> hands. Thats what it is. And the preacher's hands are in the white
> man's pockets. (Kabnis, p. 174)

Elsewhere in the story, God is seen as the creator of shopkeepers
and moralizers; Layman is portrayed as a reticent vagabond too
frightened to speak against the evils of lynching, and the singing

and shouting of a black church service are the backdrop for a chilling story of mob violence. Negative images also surround Halsey, a descendant of seven generations of shopkeepers and a man for whom time has stopped — "an old-fashioned mantelpiece supports a family clock (not running)" (p. 167). Finally, Lewis — who at different points in "Kabnis" appears as a Christ figure, a race man, and an alter ego for the protagonist — becomes "a dead chill" when confronted with the depths of the black southern experience:

> Their pain is too intense. He cannot stand it. He bolts from the table. Leaps up the stairs. Plunges through the work-shop and out into the night. (P. 226)

The most favorable assessment of Lewis that can be made is that he seems much like the narrator in "Fern" — an observer awed by the beauty and pain of the South.

The laudable characters in the play are Kabnis and Carrie K. The protagonist is the knowing artist who confronts the desert places in himself, and Carrie K. is the young, chaste ideal of a new art. Both characters, however, have their limitations. Carrie is constrained by conventional ethics:

> And then something happens. Her face blanches. Awkwardly she draws away. The sin-bogies of respectable southern colored folks clamor at her: "Look out! Be a *good* girl. A *good* girl. Look out!" (P. 205)

Kabnis is often self-indulgent, overly ceremonious, and terrified at the violence of the South. His is a Kurtzian vision, and his mulatto status (as with Paul and several of the other characters in *Cane*) comes to represent the gray world of alienation confronting modern man.

Carrie K. and Kabnis, however, are the individuals who function most effectively in the cellar, or "the hole," which represents the collective unconscious of black America. The hole is presided over by an enthroned figure whom Halsey and Carrie K. call "Father," but upon whom the awestruck Lewis bestows a religious title, "Father John." It is finally Kabnis who elicits from the black father his wisdom; the old man denounces "Th sin whats fixed

. . . upon th white folks . . . f tellin Jesus — lies. O th sin th white
folks 'mitted when they made the Bible lie" (p. 237). Carrie K.'s
reaction is one of tears and tolerance, but Kabnis — as well he
might be — is incensed. For though the old man has condemned
the hypocrisy of whites, his vocabulary is one of sin and the Bible.
Kabnis, on the other hand, knows that

> It was only a preacher's sin they [those of John's generation] knew
> in those old days, and that wasnt sin at all. Mind me, th only sin
> is whats done against th soul. Th whole world is a conspiracy t
> sin, especially in America, an against me. . . . I'm what sin is.
> (P. 236)

The protagonist is aware that a new vocabulary, one that will "fit
m soul" and capture that "twisted awful thing that crept in [to
my soul] from a dream, a godam nightmare" (p. 224), is needed;
the black man must have a new vision of life crafted by the sensitive artist. Black art can function as a new and liberating religion.

The description that begins the fifth act of "Kabnis" reinforces
this interpretation:

> Night, soft belly of a pregnant Negress, throbs evenly against the
> torso of the South. Cane — and cotton-fields, pine forests, cypress
> swamps, sawmills, and factories are fecund at her touch. Night's
> womb-song sets them singing. Night winds are the breathing of
> the unborn child whose calm throbbing in the belly of a Negress
> sets them somnolently singing. (P. 209)

This imagery is followed by the ritualistic, confessional scenes in
the hole, during which Kabnis wears a ceremonial robe; the next
morning — in a setting characterized by glowing coals and women
who have the beauty of African princesses — Kabnis prostrates
himself before John's throne. The tone of the last two acts reflects
solemnity, hope, and a new birth. Thus, when John lies expiring
in the arms of Carrie K., the scene has the significance of an
annunciation. He speaks the words "Jesus Come" in the presence
of the woman whom Lewis viewed as a mother figure for Kabnis
(p. 208) and who is described by the dramatist as "lovely in her
fresh energy of the morning, in the calm untested confidence and
nascent maternity which rise from the purpose of her present
mission" (p. 233). The concluding scene witnesses Kabnis, a

new-world creator, ascending from the cellar as the herald and agent of the dawn prophesied by Barlo in "Esther." In his hands are the dead coals of a past ritual, and the expectations generated by the opening of act 5 are fulfilled:

> Outside, the sun arises from its cradle in the tree-tops of the forest. Shadows of pines are dreams the sun shakes from its eyes. The sun arises. Gold-glowing child, it steps into the sky and sends a birth-song slanting down gray dust streets and sleepy windows of the southern town. (P. 239)

The hopes of the narrator in "Song of the Son" and the aspirations of the dreaming souls in part 2 will be realized by the initiated Kabnis, who contains the inner glow of the protagonist in "Bona and Paul" and has made a successful pilgrimage through the black heritage to the "souls of slavery."

Kabnis beseeches that he not be tortured with beauty and goes on to say, "Dear Jesus, do not chain me to myself and set these hills and valleys, heaving with folk-songs, so close to me that I cannot reach them" (p. 161). The deeper meanings of the songs have touched him, and in an early soliloquy that combines the narrator's goals in parts 1 and 2, he says: "If I, the dream (not what is weak and afraid in me) could become the face of the South. How my lips would sing for it, my songs being the lips of its soul" (p. 158). He realizes, however, that there are also inimical aspects of the past and describes them in scathing, oftentimes bitter terms. What distinguishes him from others (like Layman and Halsey, who have seen the darker side of the South) is his self-awareness; he realizes that the paranoia, aggressiveness, ambivalence, and hypocrisy of the South find counterparts in his own personality. One expects, therefore, that a portion of his new art will be devoted to serious introspection. This self-knowledge and independence lead Kabnis to recognize the profound spirit involved in the creation of the song that serves as a refrain for the drama, but they also lead him to protest bitterly the limitations implied by its lyrics:

> White-man's land.
> Niggers, sing.
> Burn, bear black children

Till poor rivers bring
Rest, and sweet glory
In Camp Ground.

Kabnis is the fully emergent artist — a singer of a displaced "soil-soaked beauty" and an agent of liberation for his people.

Cane led the way in a return to the black folk spirit, which Eugenia Collier has seen as one of the most vital developments of the Harlem Renaissance,[28] and it did so in a form and style that have scarcely been surpassed by subsequent American authors. Toomer knew — and did not attempt to sublimate — the pains and restrictions of a black southern heritage. This angst is astutely criticized in *Cane* and magnificently portrayed as the somber result of white America's exploitation and oppression, black America's too willing acceptance, and the inherent duality in the nature of man — the Manichaeanism of the universe, emblemized by the southern past — which both marvels at and seeks to destroy beauty. Opposed to "the burden of southern history" — indeed, to the darker side of human history, with its inhibitions, omnipresent violence, and moral ineptitude — however, are the pristine loveliness and indomitable spirit of the folk, to be discovered and extolled by the sensitive observer. A folk culture containing its own resonant harmonies, communal values and assumptions, and fruitful proximity to the ancestral soil offers a starting point for the journey toward black art. The artist, however, cannot simply observe the surface beauties of this culture; he must comprehend the self-knowledge and nobility of spirit that made its creation possible in the midst of an inhuman servitude. Toomer repeatedly asserts this in *Cane,* and at times the book reads like a tragic allegory, posing good against evil, suffering against redemption, hope against despair. As the reader struggles to fit the details together, he becomes increasingly involved in the complexities of the black situation. He moves, in short, toward that freedom that always accompanies deeper self-knowledge and a genuine understanding of one's condition in the universe. In this sense, *Cane* is not only a journey toward liberating black American art but also what philosophy calls the *Ding-an-sich* — the thing in itself.

II

A Many-Colored Coat of Dreams: The Poetry of Countee Cullen

When James Emanuel, who was general editor of the Broadside Critics Series, politely (and with helpful comments) suggested that "Journey toward Black Art" was unsuitable for the series, he also invited me to write an extended essay on one of the other writers of the Harlem Renaissance. Because Addison Gayle had written on the work of Claude McKay for the series and because the corpus of Langston Hughes seemed far too formidable a task for a sixty-page essay, I settled on Countee Cullen. I knew that Cullen was a controversial writer. But I also knew that controversy surrounded him because he doggedly refused to be a "Negro poet." Here, I thought, was just the test case for my critical loyalties, divided between lieder and collard greens.

For if Cullen could be redeemed by and for a Black Aesthetic, then that critical enterprise would reveal its sui generis powers of explanation. It would demonstrate, that is to say, its capacities not only of soulful ascription but also of carefully analytical description.

Since Cullen was black, a poet, and generally included in accounts of the Harlem Renaissance, the Black Aesthetic's capacity to separate the chaff of his white "pretensions" from the grain of his black "authenticity" would demonstrate the revolutionary critical mode's validity.

While I was writing "A Many-Colored Coat of Dreams," I was also attempting to find a publisher for the manuscript that eventually became *Singers of Daybreak*. One of the great disappointments of my Black Aesthetic apprenticeship was a letter from Don L. Lee (Haki Madhubuti) saying that his Third World Press could not publish the manuscript because he had decided to focus his list on "political" matters. Now if my scholarship was considered "apolitical," what precisely did the Black Aesthetic mandate? What were its criteria for effective expressive or critical commitment?

After all, Lee was a charismatic poet on the Black Arts scene in Chicago. And he could instantly transform himself from a gentle speaker of polysyllabics into an agitprop advocate for the eradication of white people. Which of his personas was "political"?

My argument in "A Many-Colored Coat of Dreams," therefore, appropriates Cullen as an occasion for reviewing my own and what I chose to conceive of as the Black Aesthetic's *dilemma*. The latent question of the essay is: What literary-critical problems and issues must be raised if the Black Aesthetic is to prove itself capable of appropriately analyzing a writer like Cullen? For Cullen was a poet whose romantic sonnets and heroic ballads were not "collards." Nevertheless, he was valorized by black readers and critics alike. I used Cullen as an occasion for testing the expressive effectiveness of the Harlem Renaissance, and the efficacy of the Black Aesthetic. I knew that Cullen was indefensible as a *black* poet according to Black Aesthetic criteria. He was not Don L. Lee, nor intended to be. But perhaps he offered the perfect occasion for accurately examining the nature of a Black Aesthetic's definition of "blackness" and other familiar signs of its project.

My recourse, then, was to *use* Cullen as a polemical challenge to the validity of the Black Aesthetic. Since he was my subject and was an unequivocal marker of one type of Harlem Renaissance "success," I claimed his work as part of the authentic ground of a black expressive tradition. Any criticism that wrote Cullen out of the record was, in my account, too political.

What were my alternatives? No viable ones, I felt.

Situated at the University of Virginia as a committed Afro-Americanist who had, quite paradoxically, been hired because he had published essays on British aestheticism, I knew that it was only insofar as the Black Aesthetic dramatically and effectively altered traditional academic criteria that it would *politically* and academically empower Afro-American academic critics. "A Many-Colored Coat of Dreams," then, is already—a bare four years after my Black Aesthetic initiation—a sign of apostasy. The essay was conditioned by a variety of personal, intellectual, and professional considerations. It was enormously difficult to write.

But it was, perhaps, the essay's difficult range of issues that makes it a far more intriguing essay on the Harlem Renaissance than "Journey toward Black Art." Yet, what was decisively missing from my approach to the poet's oeuvre was a theory of his audience. How does a seemingly "apolitical" poet such as Cullen become a bedrock of expressive cultural politics? The answer, I think, lies in the political situation and needs of the culture itself.

Cullen was celebrated by black people because he demonstrated authentic, poetical achievement to appreciative whites. He was the poetic Debi Thomas (the black woman ice skater who recently won the world championship), proving that an indisputably young, black, and talented person could be Phi Beta Kappa and write wonderful, traditional verse. I shall have more to say of such "racial" politics and their implications in Chapter 3.

 In *Caroling Dusk, An Anthology of Verse by Negro Poets,* Countee Cullen—whom one critic describes as a time-bound author raised to prominence by a white vogue[1]—gives his date of birth as May 30, 1903.[2] In that year, W. E. B. DuBois' *The Souls of Black Folk* appeared and astonished some critics with its forthright, scholarly, and hauntingly lyrical portrayal of the black American situation. Paul Laurence Dunbar, the first black American poet of distinction, had become an invalid (he died three years later of tuberculosis). *The Colonel's Dream,* released in 1905, marked the virtual end of Charles Chesnutt's career as a novelist. Though Dunbar and Chesnutt were looked upon with favor by the following generation, it was DuBois' brilliant collection that created a wave which crested during the Harlem Renaissance of the 1920s.

There is scant equivocation in *The Souls of Black Folk,* and the critic who finds no bitterness or militancy in it is simply myopic. When one probes the work, however, one finds that it is not radically out of harmony with its age. Dunbar, Chesnutt, and DuBois all wanted to be acknowledged authors, and the artistic standards they set for themselves were not far from those of the American mainstream. Chesnutt writes somewhat sentimental romances, and his letters contain a number of adulatory references to popular white American authors. DuBois' impressionistic style and his quotations from Browning, Schiller, and Swinburne display his Western orientation. And Dunbar lamented to James Weldon Johnson:

> You know, of course, that I didn't start as a dialect poet. I simply came to the conclusion that I could write it as well, if not better, than anybody else I knew of, and that by doing so I could gain a hearing. I gained the hearing, and now they don't want me to write anything but dialect.[3]

The three authors were victims of the dilemma that DuBois describes as a "double consciousness"—the black man's sense that he is both an American and something apart. When Frances E. W. Harper wrote in 1861 to the editor of a recently established periodical, "we [black authors] must look to the future which, God willing, will be better than the present or the past, and delve into the heart of the world,"[4] she captured the salient aspects of the problem. The future can always be seen as promising when one is chained to a white-dominated present, and a glance into "the heart of the world" may produce a more acceptable theme than a thoroughgoing analysis of one's oppressive situation—particularly when such an examination is likely to impress upon a white reader his own moral culpability. Simply stated, the problem is that of the black man in a white country, of the black author writing for a white public; and many thousands have perished in the resulting flood of emotions. In its more advanced form, the problem that beset DuBois, Chesnutt, and Dunbar raises an important artistic and aesthetic question. What is the task of the black American author and by what standards is he to be judged?

If this query is placed in a historical context, it is relatively easy to gaze back on turn-of-the-century America and see that the odds were stacked against the black writer who decided that he would give an unflinching portrayal of black America, that he would make no compromises, and that he — like William Lloyd Garrison — would be heard. There were simply too many Jim Crow laws and lynchings (and too few courageous publishers) for such honesty to exist. And black creativity, which was to flower in the 1920s, faced many of the same handicaps. The age that witnessed the deportation of Marcus Garvey, the heroic but unsuccessful efforts of James Weldon Johnson to secure the passage of an anti-lynching bill, and the arrest of Ossian Sweet was scarcely one of interracial harmony. Although the chronological span between the end of Dunbar's career and the publication of Countee Cullen's first volume of poetry, *Color* (1925), is almost infinitesimal, critics have seemed unable to bring these twenty years into perspective. Some make it appear that the Harlem Renaissance was a self-willed affair, springing forth from the black American consciousness like Athena from the brow of Zeus. Such writers see the 1920s as what the philosopher R. G. Collingwood calls an age of brilliance, historical evidence being abundant, and the era's major thought being accessible to human reason. It is a mistake, however, to assume that the difficulties that confronted Sutton Griggs, Charles W. Chesnutt, and W. E. B. DuBois disappeared during the 1920s as more desirable options opened for black authors.

When one breaks the shell of contemporaneity by viewing history as a series of intrinsically related events, the problems of turn-of-the-century black authors do not seem far removed from those faced by today's artists. Cataclysmic social, epistemological, and aesthetic changes do not occur with each passing decade. Paul Dunbar's "thee's" and "thou's," Countee Cullen's "albeit's" and "listeth's," Gwendolyn Brooks's polysyllabics, and Imamu Baraka's tortured and allusive verses are all intelligible within a brief historical continuum. Cultural goals and descriptive vocabularies may alter, but a dilemma such as the black American's seldom disappears in seven or eight decades.

This is not to say that art never undergoes a sudden face-lifting. William Wordsworth dealt neoclassicism a deathblow in the *Lyrical Ballads,* and T. S. Eliot made a generation aware that it had come of age (and was lost) in *The Waste Land.* But the explicit

Countee Cullen

question for the black American writer and critic — given a specific historical context (1903–73) — is how much the strategies employed by black authors from Paul Laurence Dunbar to Don L. Lee have contributed to the melioration of the black American dilemma. If the alternatives available today are equally undesirable, it seems simplistic to assert that one artistic manner has been more revolu-

tionary than another. It would be just as simplistic to assume that
the efforts of contemporary black artists alone will make the years
ahead more agreeable.

To consider art an agency of societal change is to accept certain a priori assumptions. First, one must adopt a socially oriented
critical approach, and second, one must take for granted the realistic mode as the sine qua non of artistic expression. In "Criteria
of Negro Art," DuBois approves both:

> all Art is propaganda and ever must be, despite the wailing of the
> purists. I stand in utter shamelessness and say that whatever art I
> have for writing has been used always for propaganda for gaining
> the right of black folk to love and enjoy. I do not care a damn for
> any art that is not used for propaganda. But I do care when propa-
> ganda is confined to one side while the other is stripped and silent.[5]

Like the writings of Bernard de Mandeville, Samuel Butler, and
Jean-Paul Sartre, black art is here defined in social terms; it should
conduce toward "the right . . . to love and enjoy" and must act as
a counterthrust to opposing societal patterns. The negative propaganda on one side of the "veil" described by DuBois should occasion
a resistant form of proselytizing. Inherent in this point of view is the
realistic mode, for art that provides merely vicarious escapism will
not suffice. Real human inequities have to be exposed, and proper
attitudes and values need to be molded. Art, therefore, is conceived
of as a social institution, akin to government, religion, and law.

Within this framework, Shelley's dictum that poets are the "unacknowledged legislators of the world" becomes a normative, rather
than a descriptive, statement. The poet not only puts forward the
standards that his readers are to follow but also holds up for their
admiration the struggles and individuals of the racial past that
have conformed to such standards. The aim of the artist is always
social change of a specific kind: he is concerned to bring the people
into harmony with the overall design that he — and those who have
shared in the creation of his mandate — have conceived. Such a
view approximates the nineteenth-century aesthetic statements of
Charles-Augustin Sainte-Beuve and Auguste Comte and the more
recent writings of Christopher Caudwell. Even a cursory reading
of Mao's writings on literature and art followed by a perusal of *The*

Quotable Karenga demonstrates the affinity between the doctrines of a number of socialist thinkers and the injunctions of today's nonwhite artists and aestheticians.

Black American literature came of age during the 1930s and 1940s when proletarian art was in its heyday, and Richard Wright was one of the first black American authors to achieve overwhelming national and international success. If one adds to this fact the growth of an educated black reading public, it is not difficult to understand why many writers of the fifties and sixties looked upon Wright as a paradigm for black literature and included the 1920s in the nonage of their tradition. Wright's early fiction was read approvingly by many white Americans and Europeans, and his themes and aims were often in harmony with a socialistic ideal: propagandistic, oriented toward change, and conceived in accordance with a specific social philosophy. Though the black American reaction to *Uncle Tom's Children* and *Native Son* was not entirely favorable, the National Association for the Advancement of Colored People did award Wright the Spingarn Medal in 1940; and he could feel a great deal more assurance than, say, Claude McKay or Langston Hughes in beginning their careers that black America was amenable to proletarian art.

This historical and aesthetic perspective is necessary if one is to understand the position that Countee Cullen, who was called by contemporaries the poet laureate of the Harlem Renaissance, occupies in the gallery of writers that is being contemplated by today's artists, critics, and academicians. The space assigned to Cullen seems describable as a dimly lit and seldom-visited chamber where genteel souls stare forth in benign solicitude. Darwin Turner, for example, calls him "the lost Ariel,"[6] and Nathan Huggins speaks of Cullen clinging "quite tenaciously to the genteel tradition."[7] Such phrases indicate only that Cullen did not march to the beat of the drummer who has "boomlay, boomlay, boom-layed" us into the 1970s. But critics are often embarrassed by the poet who is out of step with the age, as though someone had brought out a picture of a nonpartisan ancestor and shown it to their most committed colleagues. There follow tacit dismissals, vague apologies, and overweening defenses.

Of course, the disconcerted responses of black critics faced with the life and work of Countee Cullen are predicated upon certain progressivistic assumptions; e.g., the poet does not "lead" to the point at which black authors find themselves today. Behind these assumptions, however, lies an intention that one critic would call a corralling of the black artist into doing certain tasks;[8] there extends, in other words, the vista of social realism detailed above. Cullen did not think of art in Saint-Simonian or Caudwellian terms; his guiding mode was not the realistic but the romantic, and he believed the poet was a man in tune with higher spiritual forms rather than a social tactician. The romantic mode implies a world charged with wonder and suspends the laws of probability — there is unlimited expectation. Though piety and devotion are operative, the prevailing motive is love. Cullen's canon reflects all of these characteristics and contains the distinction between a dark romanticism of frustrated love and infidelity and a bright one of harmony and enduring friendship. The mode, or preshaping impulse, of his work is in harmony with his overall conception of the poet as a man who dwells above mundane realities; for Cullen, the poet is the dream keeper, the "man . . . endowed with more lively sensibility, more enthusiasm and tenderness," the individual who is "certain of nothing but of the holiness of the Heart's affection and the truth of Imagination." These quotations from Wordsworth and Keats are descriptive; they capture in brief the a priori mandates of the romantic poet. In *"Cor Cordium,"* "To John Keats, Poet. At Springtime," "For a Poet," "To an Unknown Poet," and "That Bright Chimeric Beast," Cullen defines the poet as a creator of immortal beauty, a man still in harmony with the mysterious and the ideal in an age "cold to the core, undeified," a person who wraps his dreams in "a silken cloth" and lays them away in "a box of gold." Such an author is far removed from the ideal social artist and can hardly be compared to many of today's black artists, who compose as though our lived realities were contingent upon their next quatrain. What we have, then, is a difference not in degree but in kind. To apply the standards of a socially oriented criticism to Countee Cullen and dismiss him is to achieve no more than a pyrrhic victory. To expect the majority of his work to consist of the type of idiomatic, foot-tapping, and right-on stanzas that mark much of the work of

Langston Hughes and Don Lee is not only naive but also disappointing. Moreover, to search always for the racial import in the writings of an artist who believed the poet dealt (or, at least, should be able to deal) above the realm of simple earthly distinctions is to find little. To examine the writings of Countee Cullen in detail, however, and attempt to understand both his aesthetic standpoint and the major ideas in his poetry is to move closer to an intelligent interpretation of both the man and the tradition to which he belongs.

The starting point of such an examination is the realization that every notable author in the black American literary tradition, Cullen included, has been dependent to some extent on the white American literary establishment—that complex of publishers, patrons, critics, scholars, journals, and reviews that can either catapult a writer to success or ignore him. The controversy between Chesnutt and DuBois over whose biography of John Brown would be allowed to make a profit for the white publisher; Chesnutt's ten-year difficulties surrounding *The House behind the Cedars;* and Paul Laurence Dunbar's bitter reaction to William Dean Howells' patronizing review of *Lyrics of Lowly Life* offer meet prototypes for today's skirmishes. Black authors in different sections of the country battle one another to secure rewards from white publishers; apparently neither James Alan McPherson nor Ralph Ellison feels the present atmosphere conducive to a second book; and Ishmael Reed ceaselessly cries forth that critics are unfair to him. When we look beyond the gaudy celebrations of black creative freedom that deluge today's market, the options available to contemporary black artists do not seem substantially increased.

The folksinger Odetta says that when she travels throughout the country she is disturbed at the criticism leveled against black people of talent by other blacks who feel they are misapplying their gifts; but she concludes that "all roads lead to Rome, and all of them must be covered." A perverse interpretation of this statement reveals its essential truth. Most paths that black artists have traveled in America *have* led to white economic gains and to the self-congratulation of the white critical establishment. On the title pages of a number of the most highly praised recent black works, one finds the familiar names — Harper, Doubleday, Harcourt, Bobbs-Merrill, etc. Moreover, the sign of success for many black American writers and critics is acknowledgment by a leading white critic, university, or newspaper.

All of this can be attributed to a system of critics and publishers that goes back to eighteenth-century Britain. And one can always list such independent black periodicals and presses as *Black World, Black Books Bulletin,* Third World Press, and Broadside Press. Neither consideration, however, carries one far from the basic premise here: during the past seventy years the situation of the black American author has remained much the same. His work has been molded largely by the white literary establishment and judged successful or unsuccessful (despite, in some instances, the vehement dissent of black America) according to the prevailing white critical standards. Any critical theory of black art that makes a one-to-one correlation between social or propagandistic art and meaningful social gains, therefore, seems absurd.

Is it not possible that the establishment has simply given us outworn codes and formulas and a few minor concessions? These not only provide an escape valve for energy that might be directed against the larger society — like that released in the ghetto riots of the sixties and the black institution building of the seventies — but also produce a confusion of aims and an immature reflection on art that result in unenlightening criticism. In this context, one might question why the collected poetry of Langston Hughes has not appeared, while his Simple books, *Not without Laughter,* and seductive titles such as *The Ways of White Folks, The Sweet Flypaper of Life,* and *The Panther and the Lash* are easily available. One would certainly want to know why Wallace Thurman's *Infants of the Spring* is not well advertised and accessible. And it is relevant to ask why there has been no reissue of the works of Countee Cullen. There seems but one possible answer: our literary tradition, like the rest of our lives, has been and is still controlled by whites to a greater extent than most are willing to admit.

Several critics who have read the books of Countee Cullen have been so confused by this situation that they have failed to provide adequate accounts of the man and his poetry. To state this, however, is not to imply that there is no insightful and productive criticism available. Indeed, such work is an integral part of the discussion that follows.

Countee Cullen (né Porter) was reared by his grandmother until he was eleven years old; when she died, he was adopted by Reverend Frederick Asbury Cullen, the pastor of Harlem's Salem Methodist Episcopal Church. The boy was given a room to himself in the quiet parsonage; and a new life of books, discussions, and parental tenderness began. The Cullens tended to overindulge their only child, but their kindness, position in the community, and trips to summer places in New Jersey and Maryland did not spoil Cullen for hard work. In both junior and senior high school, the boy was a model student, participating eagerly in extracurricular activities and bringing home commendable marks. In some ways, the adolescence of Cullen reminds one of the early life of the English poet Ernest Dowson. Like Dowson's, his summers were filled with long sheaves of verses describing his activities, and his home was characterized by a respectable frugality and industriousness. Certainly there was nothing of the pinched and nomadic wandering that beset the life of Langston Hughes. Cullen was exactly the correct young man to enter the somewhat idyllic life of Reverend and Mrs. Cullen. And it is not surprising that stories of lynchings sometimes made him physically ill or that fame early sought him out.

His first published poem, "To the Swimmer," appeared in *The Modern School* during his sophomore year at De Witt Clinton High School, and later "I have a Rendezvous with Life (with apologies to Alan Seeger)" won first prize in a competition sponsored by a women's organization. Throughout his high school career, Cullen contributed to the literary magazine and continued to hone his poetic talent. He read Paul Laurence Dunbar and the British and American romantic poets and resolved to be a writer.

After graduating from De Witt Clinton, he entered New York University, and here he came of age as a poet. He won prizes in the Witter Bynner and *Crisis* poetry contests, and by 1924 "it seemed that no literary magazine could bear to go to press without a Countee Cullen poem."[9] In the fall of 1925, Cullen entered the M.A. program at Harvard University; he came bearing fame and a Phi Beta Kappa key. During the same year, *Color* was published by Harper and Brothers, and its seventy-odd poems secured the poet's place as a leading figure of the Harlem Renaissance. The acknowledgments page—which contains such exalted names as the *American Mercury,* the *Bookman, Harper's Magazine* the *Nation,* the *Crisis,* and *Poetry*—reveals Cullen as one of the first black American poets after Dunbar to gain national celebrity.

The poet journeyed abroad with his father during the summer of 1926 and in the fall of the same year took an editorial job with *Opportunity,* the official organ of the National Urban League. In 1927, Harper released *Caroling Dusk, Copper Sun,* and Cullen's rendering of an old ballad, *The Ballad of the Brown Girl,* in single volumes. A number of critics were disappointed by *Copper Sun,* since it did not bear out the promise revealed in *Color,* but Cullen's spirits were high when he read a letter from George Lyman Kittredge describing *The Ballad of the Brown Girl* as the finest literary ballad he had ever read. The year 1928 brought further praise and a Guggenheim Fellowship. More important, it marked the year in which Cullen—with much sound and fury, enthusiasm and ado—was married to the daughter of W. E. B. DuBois. DuBois viewed the marriage of his Yolande to a "New Negro" poet as a symbolic event, a testament to the "beauty and power of a new breed of American Negro." Given the grandiloquent conceptions of DuBois, it is not surprising that the ceremony was far from a quiet and seemly affair. Nor is it striking that the couple quickly parted to attend their separate lives—Cullen in Paris and Yolande in Baltimore—and within two years firmly divorced. When he arrived in Paris, however, the young poet's prospects seemed bright. He responded as favorably to France as he had two years earlier, became associated with a group of black American artists (including Eric Walrond and Augusta Savage), and set about satisfying the expectations of the Guggenheim Foundation. Marital troubles intervened, and soon Cullen found them a constant source of distraction. His output grew smaller as his worldview grew more darkly romantic. The Guggenheim years resulted in the publication of *The Black Christ and Other Poems* in 1929 and a return to the Salem Methodist parsonage as a divorced man.

Early in the 1930s — the decade of the Great Depression that ended the Harlem Renaissance — Cullen decided to take a teaching job at Frederick Douglass Junior High School. This post turned into a career. Though *One Way to Heaven* (a novel, 1932) and *The Medea and Some Poems* (1935) both received kind reviews, by the mid-thirties Cullen's days as a serious writer were past. *The Lost Zoo* (1940) and *My Lives and How I Lost Them* (1942) are both children's books; *On These I Stand* (1947) — a collection of poems outlined before his death — contains only six previously unpublished works. Cullen died on January 10, 1946, and on Saturday, January 12, three thousand people attended his funeral at the Salem Methodist Episcopal Church.

Arna Bontemps writes:

> Cullen was in many ways an old-fashioned poet. He never ventured very far from the Methodist parsonage in which he grew up in New York. A foster child, drawn into this shelter at an early age, he continued to cherish it gratefully.[10]

Although Cullen always returned home to Harlem no matter how far he journeyed, the implications of Bontemps' statement seem questionable; the poet lived in harmony with his adopted parents and is deemed old-fashioned because he never experienced a stage of Freudian revolt. One can see how Cullen would be considered the exception in an age that brought Wallace Thurman, Bontemps himself, and a host of others from all over the country to seek fame and fortune in Harlem. Cullen was already there. Moreover, he was the first to achieve monumental success as an author and substantially to express what many of the Renaissance writers felt. Cullen is old-fashioned, I think, only to the revisionist who feels he must divide the past into neat blocks and firmly ensconce his favorites.

In many ways, the Harlem Renaissance was simply the artistic extension of the sociopolitical activities of black Americans during the 1920s. Its end was integration into the mainstream, and its means were not very different from those of white creative artists. Financial success, acknowledgment by literary figures such as H. L. Mencken, Sara Teasdale, and Witter Bynner, and the acclaim of newspapers like the *New York World* and the *Times* were considered worthy rewards by all American authors.[11] Countee Cullen was not out of step with his age when he gratefully received any of these. And unlike a number of black American authors, Cullen refused to be wooed and won by white patrons. He firmly rejected Carl Van Vechten's offer to secure a publisher for him and steadfastly refused to be channeled into a narrow stream.

Most often criticized is Cullen's choice of the romantic mode and his reliance on a long-standing poetical tradition. And if his detractors stuck to these charges, there would be little conflict. Most, however, go beyond them and assume that, say, Langston Hughes and Jean Toomer were more forthright, "modern," and independent than Cullen. To do so is to forget that the publication of Hughes's first book was contingent upon the kind offices of Vachel Lindsay, and that Toomer was—according to Marjorie Content Toomer—a man who disavowed all allegiance to the Black Renaissance.[12] The artistic independence of the black author was an implied goal rather than a tangible fact of the Renaissance, and one suspects that Cullen was not the only author who told Hughes that he wanted to be just a writer, not a "Negro" writer.[13]

In short, Cullen can be placed in the Harlem Renaissance camp that viewed the black writer's objective of universal success as one strategy for lessening the great American dilemma. To set this group at one end of the spectrum and another contingent labeled "nationalists" at the opposite end, however, is to simplify our history. The tendency to look toward the highest ideals of American society and to integrate into its common house has always been present in the minority cultures of this nation; and seldom have they contained an articulate, literate group of substantial size to publish opposition to such inclinations. For to obtain the advantage of a hearing, it has always been necessary to filter through the white man's hands, leaving behind much of the fire and independence of youthful spirit. And the men of the Harlem Renaissance were articulate, literate, and published, most having found their way through the sieve of the white world. If we call before the bench Langston Hughes, we find him starting out as a college student, a bohemian poet who turned out funky stanzas to the tune of a Park Avenue patron. Bring up Jean Toomer, and we have a genius who went unacknowledged during his day because he dared to tell the truth about the fundamental ways of black folks; this situation drove him to mysticism and whiteness. Summon Countee Cullen, and we receive a man who understood better than most the aims of his articulate black contemporaries. W. E. B. DuBois wrote:

> In a time when it is the vogue to make much of the Negro's aptitude for clownishness or to depict him objectively as a serio-comic figure, it is a fine and praiseworthy act for Mr. Cullen to show through the interpretation of his own subjectivity the inner workings of the Negro soul and mind.[14]

And Alain Locke felt that the poet blended "the simple with the sophisticated so originally as almost to put the vineyards themselves into his crystal goblets."[15] The final member of that revered Renaissance triumvirate, James Weldon Johnson, said:

> Cullen is a fine and sensitive lyric poet, belonging to the classic line. . . . He never bids for popular favor through the use of bizarre effects either in manner or subject matter. . . . All of his work is laid within the lines of the long-approved English patterns. And by that very gauge a measure of his gifts and powers as a poet may be taken. The old forms come from his hands filled with fresh beauty. A high test for a poet in this blasé age.[16]

Cullen was not destined to go unsung like Toomer nor was he subject to the kind of disillusionment that overtook Hughes. One of the most accomplished literary representatives of a majority point of view, he received both the lavish (and, at times, inordinate) praise and the ironical discomfort that accompany such a position.

With the wisdom of hindsight, one might glance back on Cullen — and the Harlem Renaissance in general — and talk of the myopia of the 1920s. Many black American artists and critics felt that the millennium had arrived. While this was certainly not true, it seems excessively critical to speak of their faulty vision. A view of Cullen's aesthetic statements reveals that one of his chief demands was the freedom of the black American artist. Like James Weldon Johnson, Cullen was interested in liberating black American poetry from the shackles of the past and in developing a strong

literary tradition. In a 1926 *Crisis* article, he writes: "I do believe
. . . that the Negro has not yet built up a large enough body of
sound, healthy race literature to permit him to speculate in abor-
tions and aberrations which other people are all too prone to
accept as truly legitimate."[17] This sounds, on the one hand, like
a Victorian moralist calling for fresh air and sunshine in art, but
it seems, on the other, wise advice to the poets of an era prone
to bizarre tangents. A firm tradition could be established only if
the writer exercised meet selectivity. Cullen says:

> Let art portray things as they are, no matter what the consequences,
> no matter who is hurt, is a blind bit of philosophy. There are some
> things, some truths of Negro life and thought, of Negro inhibi-
> tions that all Negroes know, but take no pride in. To broadcast
> them to the world will but strengthen the bitterness of our enemies,
> and in some instances turn away the interest of our friends. . . .
> *Put forward your best foot.*[18]

This enjoinder was not prescriptive, however; unlike Jessie Fauset
and others, Cullen did not believe that the field of the black artist
should be severely limited. His statement is a call for what all fine
art must possess — authorial discretion. The specific subject matter
is the choice of the individual artist:

> Must we, willy-nilly, be forced into writing nothing but the old
> atavistic urges, the more savage and none too beautiful aspects
> of our lives? May we not chant a hymn to the Sun God if we will,
> create a bit of phantasy in which not a spiritual or a blues appears,
> write a tract defending Christianity though its practitioners aid us
> so little in our argument; in short do, write, create what we will,
> our only concern being that we do it well and with all the power
> in us?[19]

This answer to a French critic who chided Cullen for employing
classical allusions and Western subject matter sounds somewhat
like Ralph Ellison's rejoinders to Irving Howe's "Black Boys and
Native Sons." But one must beware of interpreting the response
as the bourgeois artist's apology for his subjects and techniques.
Cullen never urged black writers to turn away from the ghettoes
of the land and lose themselves in learned epithets:

> The danger to the young Negro writer is not that he will find his
> aspiration in the Negro slums; I dare say there are as fine charac-
> ters and as bright dream material there as in the best strata of Negro
> society, and that is as it should be. Let the young Negro writer,
> like any artist, find his treasure where his heart lies. If the unfor-
> tunate and less favored find an affinity in him, let him surrender
> himself; only let him not pander to the popular trend of seeing
> no cleanliness in their squalor, no nobleness in their meanness and
> no common sense in their ignorance.[20]

There is condescension, but the overriding appeal here is for the
saneness of presentation, regardless of the subject matter.

Given Cullen's views on the liberty and discretion of the black
artist, it is not surprising that he considered artistic diversity a
norm in the black experience:

> The poet writes out of his experience, whether it be personal or
> vicarious, and as these experiences differ among other poets, so
> do they differ among Negro poets; for the double obligation of
> being both Negro and American is not so unified as we are often
> led to believe. A survey of the work of Negro poets will show that
> the individual diversifying ego transcends the synthesizing hue.[21]

The poet's reaction to an article by Frank Mott illustrates how
strongly he endorsed this point of view:

> Only at his [Mott's] dictum that an author *ought,* by virtue of birth
> or any other circumstance, be interested solely in any *particular*
> thing do we utter protest. The mind of man has always ridden a
> capricious wandering nag, that just will not stay reined into a beaten
> path. . . . Let us not then be stricken into such dire lamentation
> when the Negro author goes excursioning. Let the test be how much
> of a pleasant day he himself has had, and how much he has been
> enabled to impart to us.[22]

As Cullen points out, however, the black American's double
consciousness does not present a simple problem. Though he made
a strong case for the black artist's freedom from limiting categories (hoping that any merit that might reside in his own work
would "flow from it solely as the expression of a poet — with no
racial considerations to bolster it up"),[23] he found himself insensibly drawn into writing racial verse. In 1926 he said:

> In spite of myself . . . I find that I am actuated by a strong sense
> of race consciousness. This grows upon me, I find, as I grow older,
> and although I struggle against it, it colors my writing, I fear, in
> spite of everything I can do. There may have been many things
> in my life that have hurt me, and I find that the surest relief from
> these hurts is in writing.[24]

And in an interview for the *Chicago Bee* during the following year,
he said:

> Most things I write, I do for the sheer love of the music in them.
> Somehow or other, however, I find my poetry of itself treating of
> the Negro, of his joys and his sorrows — mostly of the latter, and
> of the heights and the depths of emotion which I feel as a Negro.[25]

The apologetic tone of these statements is considered gratuitous
by our own generation, but in a poet as concerned with widening
the horizons of the black author as Countee Cullen, the sentiments
are genuine. Cullen himself wanted to be an accepted poet, and
he hoped that his example and advice would lead to the instate-
ment of others in the hall of acknowledged American authors.
He realized that from one point of view his task was far from
simple:

> This question of what material the Negro writer should draw upon,
> and how he should use it, is no simon pure problem with a sure
> mathematical conclusion; it has innumerable ramifications, and
> almost all arguments can be met with a dissenting *but* equally as
> strong.[26]

One critic clarifies the reason the question was not "simon pure":
"In the twenties the Negro's gifts were still departmentalized. There
were poets in the United States, and there were Negro poets."[27]
During the 1920s (as today) the "Negro poet" was automatically
deemed inferior to "the Poet." It is one thing to say that Cullen
should never have fallen prey to such speculations; it is quite
another to realize that he was torn by the dichotomy and that in
the process of working it out he made some of the strongest statements on black artistic freedom that emerged from the Harlem
Renaissance. His apologies can surely be seen as lamentations that
America produced a kind of schizophrenia in the black artist and

made it impossible for him to translate his highest ideals into a unified and consistent body of poetry that would rank with the canons of John Keats and Percy Shelley. Moreover, they can be viewed as his painful realizations that the black man is often so scarred by his experiences in America that it is difficult for him to sustain the romantic point of view that Cullen felt most conducive to poetry. The question here is not disillusionment, but having all roads blocked from the outset. A careful reading of Cullen's aesthetic dictates reveals a man with his mind set on freedom, but one who—like the creatures in George Orwell's *Animal Farm* or like Ellison's protagonist in *Invisible Man*—was confused by the relativity of the term. The inconsistency of Cullen's canon—its peaks and deep valleys—is understandable within this context. A fine, militant racial poem is sometimes followed by popularistic verse urging a hedonistic black existence, and skillful lyrics detailing the beauty of spring precede the most trite and unimaginative stanzas on despair. Cullen was certain that he did not want to be hemmed in—that he wanted to be accepted as just a poet—but he was not sure what constituted the most daring and accomplished freedom for an American author who happened to be black. Johnson succinctly captures his situation:

> The colored poet in the United States labors within limitations which he cannot easily pass over. He is always on the defensive or the offensive. The pressure upon him to be propagandic is well nigh irresistible. These conditions are suffocating to breadth and to real art in poetry. In addition he labors under the handicap of finding culture not entirely colorless in the United States.[28]

In a headnote in *Caroling Dusk,* Cullen states that one of his chief problems was "reconciling a Christian upbringing with a pagan inclination."[29] The poems in *Color* reveal the accuracy of his comment, for a dichotomy pervades the volume. Faith and doubt, hedonism and reverence, innocence and experience, white and black, life and death are constantly juxtaposed, and the tensions that result often lead to striking poems. In the dedicatory poem, for example, "To You Who Read My Book," the brevity of existence is set against the implied immortality of the poet, and the germination of spring is seen as a foil for the destructiveness of winter:

When the dreadful Ax
  Rives me apart,
When the sharp wedge cracks
  My arid heart,
Turn to this book
  Of the singing me
For a springtime look
  At the wintry tree.[30]

And in "Tableau," Cullen uses nature imagery to demonstrate the contrast between black and white, the natural and the artificial:

Locked arm in arm they cross the way,
  The black boy and the white,
The golden splendor of the day,
  The sable pride of night.

From lowered blinds the dark folk stare,
  And here the fair folk talk,
Indignant that these two should dare
  In unison to walk.

The boys are outside, joined in the natural camaraderie of youth, while their elders—both black and white—gossip about their friendship behind lowered blinds. Bertram Woodruff has commented aptly on the bifurcation in Cullen's poetry between a cynical realism and a subjective idealism—a materialistic and a theistic conception of life[31]—and James Weldon Johnson noted the poet's sudden ironic turns of thought.[32] These are essential characteristics of the canon and grow, in part, out of the conflicts occasioned by Cullen's aesthetic stance. The poet who did not want his work bolstered by racial considerations begins *Color* with twenty-four racial poems. The artist who adopted the romantic mode is pulled continually toward the darker side of this realm, and his work abounds in pessimism and despair. Divided into four sections—"Color," "Epitaphs," "For Love's Sake," and "Varia"—*Color* expresses the major themes of the canon.

The racial poems in the volume range from the somewhat bombastic "The Shroud of Color" to the magnificently sustained and accomplished "Heritage," with a variety of noble sentiment, libertinism, atavism, fine description, and "initiation" filling out the middle range. Arthur Davis has demonstrated that one of the chief subjects of the opening section is alienation and exile:

> For Cullen, the Negro is both a geographical and a spiritual exile. He has lost not only an idyllic homeland; but equally as important, he has also lost understanding pagan gods who would be far more sympathetic to his peculiar needs than the pale Christian deities.[33]

One finds this sense of displacement in poems such as "Atlantic City Waiter," "Near White," "Brown Boy to Brown Girl," "Pagan Prayer," and "Heritage." In these poems, the black man is conceived of as a deracinated individual pulled abruptly from some Edenic place and set amidst strange gods. But there are also poems that show no sense of alienation; they simply enjoin a hedonistic existence. "To a Brown Girl," for example, offers the following comment:

> What if his glance is bold and free,
> His mouth the lash of whips?
> So should the eyes of lovers be,
> And so a lover's lips.

And "To a Brown Boy" gives similar advice:

> That brown girl's swagger gives a twitch
> To beauty like a queen:
> Lad, never dam your body's itch
> When loveliness is seen.

There are poems, moreover, that have more to do with a specific social situation than with a feeling of exile. "A Brown Girl Dead" and "Saturday's Child" are both ironical protests against economic depression:

> Her mother pawned her wedding ring
> To lay her out in white;
> She'd be so proud she'd dance and sing
> To see herself tonight.
>
> ("A Brown Girl Dead")

For I was born on Saturday—
　"Bad time for planting a seed,"
Was all my father had to say,
　And, "One mouth more to feed."

Death cut the strings that gave me life,
　And handed me to Sorrow,
The only kind of middle wife
　My folks could beg or borrow.

("Saturday's Child")

The dominant feeling of the racial poems, however, is (in the words of Claude McKay) one of being "born, far from my native clime, / Under the white man's menace, out of time."

"Yet Do I Marvel" and "Heritage" capture the irony and ambiguity of this situation. The former is devastating in its restrained cynicism:

I doubt not God is good, well-meaning, kind,
And did He stoop to quibble could tell why
The little buried mole continues blind,
Why flesh that mirrors Him must some day die.

The list of incongruities moves to the assertion that God's ways are too grandiose for the simple human mind; then, with a swift stroke of genius, come the concluding lines:

Yet do I marvel at this curious thing:
To make a poet black, and bid him sing!

The angst of Cullen's aesthetic is summed up in this couplet. By association, the black poet takes on the burdens of the disinherited and is doomed to the tortures of Sisyphus and Tantalus; the persona exposes both his own skepticism and the awesome task of the black artist.

"Heritage" displays the same sense of irony and skepticism. The poem opens with what turns out to be a rhetorical question:

What is Africa to me:
Copper sun or scarlet sea,
Jungle star or jungle track,

> Strong bronzed men, or regal black
> Women from whose loins I sprang
> When the birds of Eden sang?

The text reveals that Africa is not only the spirit realm to which the narrator feels most allied but also a land in fierce opposition to his present home. As in McKay's "Flame-Heart," the narrator in "Heritage" makes a claim that is not justified by the poem itself:

> Africa? A book one thumbs
> Listlessly, till slumber comes.
> Unremembered are her bats
> Circling through the night, her cats
> Crouching in the river reeds,
> Stalking gentle flesh that feeds
> By the river brink.

The vivid descriptions of its fierce flowers and pagan impulses show that Africa is much more than bedtime reading for the narrator. Moreover, when he states that he is trying to move beyond the call of heathen deities, the text leaps forth in refutation. Some critics have faulted Cullen for "Heritage," stating that he makes topographical mistakes and perpetuates the idea of the black man as a "noble savage."[34] Such responses can carry one only so far, however, with a poem as thoroughly ironical as "Heritage." While it is true that there is an undue enthusiasm recurrent in the passages on Africa, it is also true that Cullen was interested in a blatant contrast between the benign and unsmiling deities of the new land and the thoroughly initiated gods of the old. The entire poem is placed in a confessional framework as the narrator tries to define his relationship to some white, ontological being and finds that a black impulse ceaselessly draws him back. The italicized concluding lines read like the penance exacted from an unregenerate schoolboy:

> *All day long and all night through,*
> *One thing only must I do*
> *Quench my pride and cool my blood,*
> *Lest I perish in the flood,*
> *Lest a hidden ember set*

Timber that I thought was wet
Burning like the dryest flax,
Melting like the merest wax,
Lest the grave restore its dead.
Not yet has my heart or head
In the least way realized
They and I are civilized.

"Heritage" is a longer and more comprehensive statement of the message contained in "Pagan Prayer," and it reveals the sharp line that Cullen saw dividing two cultures. The poet's "paganism" reveals itself in the end as a repudiation of the white man's religion.

A poem like "Incident" reveals why such a rejection is necessary:

Once riding in old Baltimore,
    Heart-filled, head-filled with glee,
I saw a Baltimorean
    Keep looking straight at me.

Now I was eight and very small,
    And he was no whit bigger,
And so I smiled, but he poked out
    His tongue, and called me, "Nigger."

I saw the whole of Baltimore
    From May until December;
Of all the things that happened there
    That's all that I remember.

The sense of irony and the dichotomized worldview that appear throughout Cullen's work are skillfully captured here. There is a movement from gay innocence to initiation,[35] which is repeated in the seasonal reference ("May until December"), and at the time of recounting the speaker has not forgotten the incident. Not only the vistas of Baltimore, one suspects, but the whole of his life has been clouded by the sudden realization that the norms of the larger society do not work for him. Adjustment often involves the type of repudiation seen in "Heritage" and "Pagan Prayer."

The two themes that stand out in *Color*'s nonracial poems are love and mortality. The second section consists of twenty-nine epitaphs written in the manner of Edgar Lee Masters' *Spoon River Anthology*. Cullen, however, is not interested in showing what the restrictions of the village do to the human psyche. He is concerned with the many types that make up society, and thus the poems display subtle irony, tender feeling, and adept portraiture. "For a Lady I Know" captures in miniature the type of woman whom the poet's atavistic "Atlantic City Waiter" might have served:

> She even thinks that up in heaven
>> Her class lies late and snores,
> While poor black cherubs rise at seven
>> To do celestial chores.

"For My Grandmother" demonstrates Cullen's ability to set forth mild sentiments:

> This lovely flower fell to seed;
>> Work gently, sun and rain;
> She held it as her dying creed
>> That she would grow again.

There is fine irony in both "For a Virgin" and "For an Atheist":

> For forty years I shunned the lust
>> Inherent in my clay;
> Death only was so amorous
>> I let him have his way.

and

> Mountains cover me like rain,
>> Billows whirl and rise;
> Hide me from the stabbing pain
>> In His reproachful eyes.

Finally, there is the often quoted "For Paul Laurence Dunbar":

> Born of the sorrowful of heart,
>> Mirth was a crown upon his head;
> Pride kept his twisted lips apart
>> In jest, to hide a heart that bled.

Though the poems as a group offer a comment on various styles of human life, the overwhelming fact of the sequence — as of all epitaphs — is the common end to which flesh is heir. This common end is the source of much of the humor that resides in the individual sketches, and the same sense of mortality occasions the despair that appears in a number of the poems in the concluding sections of *Color*.

It may seem commonplace to say that Cullen's romanticism is derivative, but in the context of nineteenth-century English poetry the statement becomes more descriptive. Though the poet chose as his ideal the second wave of British romanticism, including Keats and Shelley, his own lyrics read more like the work of Dante Rossetti, Charles Swinburne, and the authors of fin de siècle England. These were the romantics manqué who shared the same lyrical impulses but lacked the sweeping vision, the mythicizing potential, and the colossal certainties of their predecessors. The shades of Ernest Dowson and Arthur Symons appear with the first lines of "Oh, for a Little While Be Kind":

> Oh, for a little while be kind to me
> Who stand in such imperious need of you,
> And for a fitful space let my head lie
> Happily on your passion's frigid breast.

The moment of contentment is brief, and though the poem ends on an ironical note, its basic assumptions are that life is fleeting and love is short. "If You Should Go" deals once again with the departure of the beloved, and "To One Who Said Me Nay" is a restatement of the familiar carpe diem theme. "Advice to Youth" follows the same pattern, while "Caprice" captures the heartrending and incomprehensible ways of love:

> "I'll tell him, when he comes," she said,
>   "Body and baggage, to go,
> Though the night be darker than my hair,
>   And the ground be hard with snow."
>
> But when he came with his gay black head
>   Thrown back, and his lips apart,
> She flipped a light hair from his coat,
>   And sobbed against his heart.

Once again we see the contrasts that mark Cullen's verse — harmony and discontent, light and dark. Both "Sacrament" and "Bread and Wine" as one might expect juxtapose the sacred and the profane. In the first, the speaker is considered unworthy of the beloved; in the second, the beloved is deemed the only thing holy in a mortal world. Cullen's use of religious imagery in the two poems is in harmony with his canon as a whole, for time and again there are biblical allusions.[36] The final poem in the third section, "Spring Reminiscence," moves quite well until the final couplet, where the merger of a religious allusion with a colloquialism destroys the effect. The poem, however, has thematic significance, for it is a memory in spring of springs gone by. There is the possibility, in other words, of resurrecting the joy and beauty of the past through the agency of poetry. The poet and his experiences possess a certain immortality, and spring — the time of nature's rejuvenation — becomes symbolic of enduring spirituality.

All of this cannot be inferred from "Spring Reminiscence," of course, but the stanza quoted earlier from "To You Who Read My Book," combined with "In Memory of Col. Charles Young" and "To John Keats, Poet. At Springtime," makes the argument clearer. Young, the black colonel who was forced to retire from the army at the beginning of World War I to prevent his promotion to general, becomes one with nature in the course of the poem:

> The great dark heart is like a well
>   Drained bitter by the sky,
> And all the honeyed lies they tell
>   Come there to thirst and die.
>
> No lie is strong enough to kill
>   The roots that work below;
> From your rich dust and slaughtered will
>   A tree with tongues will grow.

And there is a similar merger and generative process in "To John Keats, Poet. At Springtime":

> And you and I, shall we lie still,
> John Keats, while Beauty summons us?
> Somehow I feel your sensitive will

Is pulsing up some tremulous
Sap road of a maple tree, whose leaves
Grow music as they grow, since your
Wild voice is in them, a harp that grieves
For life that opens death's dark door.
Though dust, your fingers still can push
The Vision Splendid to a birth,
Though now they work as grass in the hush
Of the night on the broad sweet page of the
    earth.

Part of Cullen's "pagan inclination" displays itself in poems like these, where he not only reminds us of the ineluctability of the spiritual but also recalls the fact that spring (before its arrogation by Christianity) was a time of bacchanalian celebration and heady splendor in the grass. For the poet, spring is the season when the natural man, the sensitive soul, and the germinating seed push forth in a rebirth of wonder.

    Finally in *Color* are Cullen's concern for the outcast — "Black Magdalens," "For Daughters of Magdalen," and "Judas Iscariot" — and his treatment of the idealistic dreamer. The poet achieves a masterful irony by placing streetwalkers in a biblical context:

They fare full ill since Christ forsook
    The cross to mount a throne,
And Virtue still is stooping down
    To cast the first hard stone.

and

Ours is the ancient story:
    Delicate flowers of sin,
Lilies, arrayed in glory,
    That would not toil nor spin.

Judas is viewed as a man who had to betray Christ so the vision He cherished would come true. In "Simon the Cyrenian Speaks," the persona says:

But He was dying for a dream,
    And He was very meek,

And in His eyes there shone a gleam
  Men journeyed far to seek.

In "For a Poet," the creative artist is also viewed as a keeper of
dreams. Like other matter in Cullen's canon, therefore, Christianity is seen in a dual light. Insofar as God is cryptic or
inscrutable in *Color*'s first two poems, He is the object of cynicism
and repudiation; as Christ, the carrier of the dream, however,
He is to be ranked among the highest idealists.

"I've kept on doing the same things, and doing them no better.
I have never gotten to the things I really wanted to do," Dunbar
told James Weldon Johnson as he suffered the agonies of his final
illness.[37] Some would expect a similar confession from Countee
Cullen, since *Color* is his finest volume, although he went on to produce four more. If the poet had made a similar statement, he would
have falsified his own accomplishments. Some things he did a good
deal better as his career progressed. From his early efforts, he
moved to the fine group of poems labeled "Interlude" in *The Black
Christ,* and he developed his narrative voice in *The Ballad of the
Brown Girl.* He not only provided a rendering of Euripides' *Medea*
but also did work as a translator. And in his final volume, he seems
to counteract — through the sanity and balance of his verse — Benjamin Brawley's charge that "there is a sophomoric note in the
work of Mr. Cullen that he finds it hard to outgrow."[38]

The overriding dichotomy in the second volume, *Copper Sun,*
is one of stasis and change.[39] On the one hand, the poet believes
despair is enduring and death the bitter end of all. On the other,
he sees a better day approaching, the possibility of regeneration
and immortality, and death as an occasion for solace and wisdom.
The seven racial poems in *Copper Sun* fall generally on the positive side. Though he is now battered and scarred, there is a new
day coming for the black American:

We shall not always plant while others reap
The golden increment of bursting fruit,
Not always countenance, abject and mute,
That lesser men should hold their brothers
    cheap.

("From the Dark Tower")

If for a day joy masters me,
Think not my wounds are healed;
. . . .
They shall bear blossoms with the fall;
I have their word for this,
Who tend my roots with rains of gall,
And suns of prejudice.

("Confession")

Our flesh that was a battle-ground
Shows now the morning-break;
The ancient deities are downed
For Thy eternal sake.
Now that the past is left behind,
Fling wide Thy garment's hem
To keep us one with Thee in mind,
Thou Christ of Bethlehem.

("The Litany of the Dark People")

The metaphor of germination appears (particularly in "Threnody for a Brown Girl"), and the last poem in the group seems to favor an acceptance of the white man's religion as a means of salvation. Despite the laconic warning of Uncle Jim that "White folks is white," the speaker in most of the poems has adopted the attitude that improvement is a reality for the black American. There are tones of apocalypse in both "From the Dark Tower" and "Confession," but "The Litany of the Dark People" does much to soften them.

The optimism of the first section is out of harmony with the remainder of *Copper Sun,* for a note of despondency sounds with "Pity the Deep in Love." And while there is a contrapuntal rhythm between this and the poems that speak of the eternality of beauty and the splendor of the dream, the pervasive timbre is melancholy:

Pity the deep in love;
They move as men asleep
Traveling a narrow way
Precipitous and steep.

("Pity the Deep in Love")

But never past the frail intent
My will may flow,
Though gentle looks of yours are bent
Upon me where I go.

So much I, starved for love's delight,
Affect the mute,
When love's divinest acolyte
Extends me holy fruit.

("Timid Lover")

Of all men born he deems himself so much
    accurst,
His plight so piteous, his proper pain so
    rare,
The very bread he eats so dry, so fierce his
    thirst,
What shall we liken such a martyr to?
    Compare
Him to a man with poison raging in his
    throat
And far away the one mind with an
    antidote.

("Portrait of a Lover")

The unrequited love, dejection, indifference, carpe diem, and sighing in *Copper Sun* would have delighted the nineteenth-century decadent poets and were enough to stimulate anew the pale shades of Sir John Suckling and Edmund Waller. Cullen's songs of desperation in the second volume do not seem to have a substantial base; somehow they come across as exercises in depression rather than genuine reflections of the poet's inner being. It is, of course, difficult to argue about the effect a poem has on the reader, and one should steer clear of Wimsatt and Beardsley's "affective fallacy"—contemplating a poem as though it were the ground for some ultimate emotional state.[40] What heightens one's impression of insincerity, however, is the body of poems that state exactly the opposite point of view.

The lovers' relationship may not terminate entirely, and there is always a nagging hope in the background:

What if you come
Again and swell
The throat of some
Mute bird;
How shall I tell?
How shall I know
That it is so,
Having heard?

("Words to My Love")

Come, let us plant our love as farmers
    plant
A seed, and you shall water it with tears,
And I shall weed it with my hands until
They bleed. Perchance this buried love
    of ours
Will fall on goodly ground and bear a tree
With fruit and flowers

("The Love Tree")

Though love departs, its beauty may either linger or be reborn.
And this ambiguity is also present in the poet's treatment of death.
In "To Lovers of Earth: Fair Warning" he states that man's end
is certain and that it goes unmarked by nature. In the following
poem, "In Spite of Death," however, the speaker says:

No less shall I in some new fashion flare
Again, when death has blown my candles out;
Although my blood went down in shameful rout
Tonight, by all this living frame holds fair,
Though death should closet me tonight, I swear
Tomorrow's sun would find his cupboard bare.

In "Cor Cordium," "The Poet," and "To Endymion," Cullen once
again views the poet and his song as immortal, and he further
confuses the issue with "Hunger" and "At the Wailing Wall in Jeru-
salem," where he views both dreams and the holy wall as tokens
of everlasting beauty.

The question is not one of arrangement in Copper Sun; no new
scheme would alter the content of the individual poems. Cullen
seems to have been confronted with the problem of choosing

between alternatives. The smaller number of racial poems is an indication that he had decided to steer closer to the universal romantic ideal, but the prevailing dichotomy and the issue of "belief in poetry" that the volume raises give evidence that he had not found a firm base on which to stand as a romantic poet. He laments, derides, and protests the passing of love and life but never faces the issues of despair and mortality in a convincing manner. One suspects that Harvey Webster had *Copper Sun* very much in mind when he wrote: "Cullen neither accepted nor developed a comprehensive world-view. As a consequence his poems seem to result from occasional impulses rather than from directions by an integrated individual."[41] Of course, one knows that Cullen was anything but an "integrated individual" and that the bifurcations in his weltanschauung result, in part, from his aesthetic stance. They play an important role in *Color.* In the second volume, however, the division between stasis and change is accompanied by a narrowing of range and blatant contradictions that cause one to think back on Brawley's statement with a smile of assent.

The Ballad of the Brown Girl, An Old Ballad Retold makes much more effective use of the divisions that are basic to Cullen's poetry.[42] The narrator insists that the story was garnered from the grandams "in the land where the grass is blue," and it is not surprising that an English ballad should find its way into the repertoire of a Kentucky storyteller, since some regions of that state were at one time considered the finest preserves of Elizabethan dialect. What is striking is the interpretation that Cullen places on the ballad. Rather than a story of a "dark brown" peasant contending with a fair city maiden for the heart of an aristocrat, Cullen presents a small and colorful drama of miscegenation and conflict. The leitmotif and moral involve the dangers of the acquisitive instincts, and Lord Thomas's mother is left with the burden of the guilt. Cullen shows himself a master of the ballad stanza in the poem, and his unique rendering of the tale makes it possible for him to engage in fine color imagery:

> Her hair was black as sin is black
> And ringed about with fire;
> Her eyes were black as night is black

When moon and stars conspire;
Her mouth was one red cherry clipt
In twain, her voice a lyre.

or

Her skin was white as almond milk
Slow trickling from the flower;
Her frost-blue eyes were darkening
Like clouds before a shower.

There are several things that mar the poem. First, the hero is
a pale and nervous specter when the ballad opens, a man who
must kneel before his mother to learn which woman to choose.
At the end, he is a farseeing individual capable of an ennobling
suicide. T. S. Eliot's reservations about Hamlet might well apply
to Lord Thomas. Second, Cullen — after a skillful dramatic build-
up and climax — relies upon description for his denouement.
Finally, the ascription of guilt to the mother seems simplistic, as
do the morals of most ballads. Cullen could have mined his material, however, for a more complex statement of the issues his interpretation raises. There are also several infelicities of style.

The Black Christ and Other Poems represents a marked progression in Cullen's thought.[43] The volume closes rather than opens with
a section titled "Color," and the beginning "Varia" group makes
a number of definite statements about the poet and the age in which
he lives. In "To the Three for Whom the Book," the speaker is the
committed, romantic poet — the man who dwells above the bending
of an "idolatrous knee" to stone and steel. He is the individual who
writes of "old, unhappy, far-off things, / And battles long ago."
"That Bright Chimeric Beast" reinforces the point:

That bright chimeric beast
Conceived yet never born,
Save in the poet's breast,
The white-flanked unicorn,
Never may be shaken
From his solitude;
Never may be taken
In any earthly wood.

There is lost love and despondency in *The Black Christ,* but the volume also expresses a sincerity and a certainty about the artist's task that are lacking in *Copper Sun.* In "To an Unknown Poet" the dreamer is removed from an unholy time, and in "Counter Mood" the speaker asserts his own immortality. "A Miracle Demanded" comes as a surprise from the poet who marched to a pagan drummer in *Color;* he now asks for a renewal of his faith and a confirmation of the position taken in "Counter Mood." Finally, there are poems like "A Wish," "Minutely Hurt," and "Self-Criticism" that show a movement toward a more balanced view of life. In "Minutely Hurt," there is little of the dire lamentation of the rejected lover, and the other two poems express the poet's hope that when he has had his say he will possess the wisdom and courage to stop writing. Meanwhile, the dreamer's life remains one of commitment and loneliness:

> The poet is compelled to love his star,
> Not knowing he could never tell you why
> Though silence makes inadequate reply.
>
> ("Tongue-tied")

> A hungry cancer will not let him rest
> Whose heart is loyal to the least of dreams;
> There is a thorn forever in his breast
> Who cannot take his world for what it seems;
> Aloof and lonely must he ever walk
> Plying a strange and unaccustomed tongue,
> An alien to the daily round of talk,
> Mute when the sordid songs of earth are sung.
>
> ("A Thorn Forever in the Breast")

The sense of maturity and dedication in *The Black Christ* results, first, from the marital difficulties Cullen was encountering when a number of the poems were written. Second, the volume was composed in France, and it is possible that Cullen felt he could be "just a poet" there:

> As he whose eyes are gouged craves light
>   to see,
> And he whose limbs are broken strength
>   to run,

So have I sought in you that alchemy
That knits my bones and turns me to the
    sun;
And found across a continent of foam
What was denied my hungry heart at home.

> ("To France," from *The Medea and Some Poems*)

Third, when *The Black Christ* was published, he had tentatively
resolved the problem of a Christian background and a pagan
inclination.

"Interlude," the section that deals with the termination of a
love affair, constitutes one of the most unified and consistent
groups of Cullen's poetry, and its careful style and unfeigned sim-
plicity are akin to George Meredith's *Modern Love*. Two poems
capture the spirit and the mastery of the group:

I know of all the words I speak or write,
Precious and woven of a vibrant sound,
None ever snares your faith, intrigues you
    quite,
Or sends you soaring from the solid ground.
You are the level-headed lover who
Can match my fever while the kisses last,
But you are never shaken through and through;
Your roots are firm after the storm has
    passed.
I shall know nights of tossing in my sleep
Fondling a hollow where a head should lie;
But you a calm review, no tears to weep,
No wounds to dress, no futile breaths to
    sigh.
Ever this was the way of wind with flame:
To harry it, then leave swift as it came.

> ("The Simple Truth")

Breast under breast when you shall lie
    With him who in my place
Bends over you with flashing eye
    And ever nearing face;

Hand fast in hand when you shall tread
  With him the springing ways
Of love from me inherited
  After my little phase;

Be not surprised if suddenly
  The couch of air confound
Your ravished ears upbraidingly,
  And silence turn to sound.

But never let it trouble you,
  Or cost you one caress;
Ghosts are soon sent with a word or two
  Back to their loneliness.

("Ghosts")

Cullen thus deals with the most genuine and heartrending emotions he had ever felt, and in the volume's final poem he constructs his strongest assertion of faith.

"The Black Christ (Hopefully dedicated to White America)" is the story of a lynching in which Christ mysteriously appears and offers himself for the intended victim. The poem traces the narrator's movement from doubt to faith and depicts his mother as an archetypal southern black American who holds to the ideals of Christianity. To view the poem as simply the story of a rebellious and agnostic Jim who strikes down a white man and is condemned to death by a mob, however, is to do it less than justice. And, in a sense, to treat the poem as a simple resolution of the narrator's uncertainties is to fail to comprehend its significance in Cullen's canon. On its most fundamental level, "The Black Christ" fits into the tradition of black American literature as a conversion tale; it is one of those recountings — complete with mysterious events and marvelings at the Lord's way — that characterized the black church during Reconstruction and that can be heard today when the out-of-town guest is called upon to "testify." Cullen captures the spirit of these occasions quite well in *One Way to Heaven,* and there is little doubt that the son of a successful Harlem minister was familiar with conversion stories. If the poem is seen in this light, some of its apparent flaws turn out to be necessities, e.g., the long retelling of incidents and the sense of suspense and wonder the narrator attempts to create toward the conclusion. A man speaking to a congregation would be remiss in not accounting for every detail and strange phenomenon.

Cullen seems to adopt the form of the conversion story in a rather tentative way, however, for Jim — the agnostic badman hero — certainly appears as glamorous as the sacrificial Christ. But surely this was intentional, since the final reconciliation represents a momentary stasis in the Christian-pagan conflict. Jim, after all, commits his assault because the white man has corrupted the natural reverence for spring on the part of the black man and white woman, and the virginal tree on which Christ is hung comes to life after the lynching. Christ (the representative of religious faith) and Jim — the sensitive, agnostic worshiper of spring — come together in a rite of regeneration. In the pagan and natural moment, Jim and the white woman are as harmonious as the boys in "Tableau." The white man intrudes, and he and the mob stand for white America. The narrator never loses his admiration for his brother, and the wonder and firmness he feels in his new faith are the results of a miracle.

Throughout the poem, Cullen seems to stand by the narrator's side, whispering that both Christ, the dreamer, and the pagan-spirited Jim are needed to unify the opposing points of his canon. To say the poet avoids some of the issues — like Christ's exoneration of a murderer and the hopelessness His crucifixion portends — is to capture the letter of the poem, but not its spirit. It was inevitable that Cullen would attempt a synthesis and that he would do so in a manner that raised the question of race. The results are not altogether satisfactory, but the strong commitment to an idealistic point of view should not be forgotten. The poet, the dreamer, the man who treasures the wonders of spring wins out in the end. If culture was not entirely "colorless" in the United States, at least it was neutral enough in France for Cullen to compose his only truly romantic volume of poetry. The book contains the poet's message "To Certain Critics":

> Then call me traitor if you must,
> Shout treason and default!

Say I betray a sacred trust
Aching beyond this vault.
I'll bear your censure as your praise,
For never shall the clan
Confine my singing to its way
Beyond the ways of man.

No racial option narrows grief,
Pain is no patriot,
And sorrow plaits her dismal leaf
For all as lief as not.
With blind sheep groping every hill,
Searching an oriflamme,
How shall the shepherd heart then thrill
To only the darker lamb?

Six years elapsed between *The Black Christ* and *The Medea and Some Poems,* Cullen's last volume of serious verse.[44] The prose rendering of Euripides' classic play is interesting and shows a broadening of the poet's activities, but it possesses little of the grandeur of the original. Cullen added two female characters to the drama to act as confidantes for Medea; in Euripides' version, the entire chorus acts the role. The substitution means that one of the Greek dramatist's major contentions loses much of its force; no longer is a large sector of the city-state inclined toward the irrationality and paganism represented by the heroine. There seems little possibility that the entire order will be destroyed by the kind of wild frenzy that characterizes the *Bacchae.* Cullen's work is also more maudlin than Euripides'. Medea's soliloquy over her victims and the words of one of her children before the execution—"What are you such a baby for? Mother won't hurt us. Ah!"—drip with sentimentality. Finally, Cullen's characters speak far too often in Poor Richard slang, and his heroine is reduced to a shrew who engages in such incongruously comical exchanges as:

Medea: Then you have no sons yet, Aegeus?
Aegeus: None. The gods have kept me barren!
Medea: Have you tried a wife? That might help.

Cullen's effort precedes Jean-Paul Sartre's rendition of Aeschylus by a number of years. But Sartre's *The Flies* was undertaken as an act of freedom and was first performed in occupied Paris. Hence, there is more justification for his deliberately second-rate translation; it offers an example of "engaged" literature. Cullen's play suffers by comparison, for it shifts the emphasis from the mythic, barbarian, and fatalistic in the original to the hard-hearted woman scorned. Certainly this aspect is present in the Euripidean version, but it is not blatant. Cullen's flaccid prose and rhyming choruses are scarcely improvements on earlier translations.

The twenty-eight lyrics in *The Medea and Some Poems* make the volume readable and show a mellowing of the poet's attitudes and a refinement of his technique. There is an expansion of his humanism in verses such as "Magnets," "Any Human to Another," "Every Lover," and "To One Not There," and he rededicates himself to poetry in "After a Visit (At Padraic Colum's where there were Irish poets)." His sonnet "Some for a little while do love" and the concluding poems show a movement toward a more controlled verse and a more gentle (one might almost say "senescent") point of view:

Some for a little while do love, and some
    for long;
And some rare few forever and for aye;
Some for the measure of a poet's song,
And some the ribbon width of a summer's
    day.
Some on a golden crucifix do swear,
And some in blood do plight a fickle troth;
Some struck divinely mad may only stare,
And out of silence weave an iron oath.

So many ways love has none may appear
The bitter best, and none the sweetest
    worst;
Strange food the hungry have been known
    to bear,
And brackish water slakes an utter thirst.

It is a rare and tantalizing fruit
Our hands reach for, but nothing
   absolute.

"To France" asks that the land of "kindly foreign folk" act as the poet's Byzantium, and "Belitis Sings (From the French of Pierre Louys)" is charming in its delicate artificiality. Finally, "The Cat" and "Cats"—both translations of Baudelaire—substitute the feline loveliness of a domestic pet for the mythical beasts and fickle lovers seen elsewhere in Cullen's canon. Cats are "quiet as scholars and as lovers bold," and they sit "in noble attitudes" and dream—"small sphinxes miming those in lonelier lands." The poet thus sinks quietly into a land of domesticity with a cat for his companion.

The volume closes, however, with "Scottsboro, Too, Is Worth Its Song," a protest poem on the order of "Not Sacco and Vanzetti" (*The Black Christ*). Though Cullen would, henceforth, live and write in collaboration with his cherished Christopher Cat, "all disgrace" and "epic wrong" still exercise their ineluctable and dichotomizing influence. The man who was born black and bidden to sing turned to the world of children for his next two books, but his canon closes on the propagandistic note that James Weldon Johnson found "well nigh irresistible" for the black artist.

Countee Cullen never achieved the "Vision Splendid." He can be classified as a minor poet whose life and poetry raise major problems. If we condemn him for his lack of independence and his rise to fame through the agency of noted American critics and periodicals, we are forced to do the same for a host of others. If he is judged and sentenced to exile on the basis of his aesthetic, a number of excellent statements on the black artist's tasks and difficulties are lost. If he is upbraided for his lack of directness and his reliance on a longstanding tradition, our evaluation of the entire corpus of black American poetry must be modified. It is possible that we are now whirling about fiercely in the maelstrom of a black poetic revolution, but a careful view of Countee Cullen brings doubt. There is much continuity between the career of the Harlem Renaissance poet and the generations that have followed. As one glances from Cullen to present works and back, it is sometimes hard to tell the difference. In short, Cullen offers a paradigm of the black American creative experience, and summary appraisals of his work lead to obfuscation rather than the clarity we so sorely need. He wrote a number of outstanding romantic lyrics and contributed racial poems that will endure because they grant insight into the black American dilemma. But perhaps it is fitting to allow his own guiding star to render the final judgment. John Keats defined our wisest stance toward Cullen when he wrote:

> Men should bear with each other—there lives not the Man who may not be cut up, aye hashed to pieces on his weakest side. The best of Men have but a portion of the good in them—a kind of spiritual yeast in their frames which creates the ferment of existence —by which a Man is propell'd to act and strive and buffet with Circumstance. The sure way . . . is first to know a Man's faults, and then be passive, if after that he insensibly draws you towards him then you have no Power to break the link.[45]

 **III**

Lowground and Inaudible Valleys: Reflections on Afro-American Spirit Work

The implicit claim of the following essay is that only an inventive negotiation of the spiritual depths of black expressivity provides a common geography for Jean Toomer, Countee Cullen, Amiri Baraka, Larry Neal, and Hoyt Fuller. The creation of such a geography requires an informed faith in Afro-American spirit work — in the ceaseless and, indeed, poetic flow of an impulse that both unifies Afro-American life and history and makes them coherent.

"Informed" is the key word. For it suggests ceaseless reading, listening, observation, revision, expansion, and correction as processes that enable a critic to know, for example, that "chilling" does not refer to wine. The example suggests that "informed" includes requisite attention to the vernacular — to everyday social and political realities. Such attention is an indispensable complement to archival research and scholarly reading.

What dawned on me quite early in my study of Afro-American expressive culture was the realization that scholars like Stephen Henderson and Vincent Harding were far ahead of me as cultural analysts because they were already attuned to the vernacular. Henderson's deep knowledge of black music and Harding's consummate command of the magisterial style and oratory of the black preacher fitted them out with a kind of immediate access to resonances and tonalities of black cultural texts that I came to hear only in mediated ways — notably, through Harding's and Henderson's scholarly lectures, books, and essays.

I remember how captivated I was — even during my Yale days — by Harding's inspiring, early-morning television lectures on black history. Similarly, I remember a heady feeling of achieved cultural wisdom after reading Stephen Henderson's *Understanding the New Black Poetry.* Henderson's work provided a sharp, black, revisionary swerve from Brooks and Warren's *Understanding Poetry;* it became a kind of poetical scripture in its own right — a spiritual chronicle of the "def" groundations of a musical and idiomatic poetical tradition.

More than simply "informed," however, scholars like Harding, Henderson, and Hoyt Fuller had *faith* in the ultimate significance of the vernacular. Which is to say, they had an explicit and unshakable trust in the value of their *own* explicitly racial instincts and experiences. They entertained no doubts about the absolute necessity to allow the spirit of a culture's expressive genius to dictate the form and guide the presentation and purpose of their own work. In a word, they never thought of themselves as "just scholars," but rather as scholars who would gladly say with Run-DMC: "Well you know I'm proud to be black." How to achieve such energy, style, and faith was not altogether clear to me a decade ago.

Gradually, however, I realized that the trick was to relinquish illusions such as the fantasy common among black intellectuals that white academics are guided in their interaction with black intellectuals by "nonracial" criteria. The fantasy plays itself out in slow frames. Its black champions dream of the black scholar as the subject of a *serious* conversation among the best and brightest whites in his or her field. The word "Nigger" — in the fantasy — is never uttered, or implied.

Black intellectuals, I think, are fairly sure that the rules of the academic game are racially fixed. Nonetheless, in their efforts to preserve illusion, they commit themselves to "working harder" in order to meet "standard" criteria. Sometimes, however, they expend so much energy apprehensively listening for disillusioning racial categorizations that they scarcely have a moment to heed the redemptive, racial sounds of the only life they will ever be able to claim in the United States.

I have tried to indicate how my allegiance to standard critical procedures and norms led to confusion. To detail fully the manner in which I minimized cognitive dissonance and literary-critical confusion would require far too much space. I can briefly say, however, that my nationalistic determination to appropriate an array of "standard" disciplines to the task of building a vernacular theory of Afro-American expressive culture taught me that some of the most able scholars of linguistics, history, anthropology, psychology, and philosophy are advocates for the determinative role of interpretation in *all* scholarly work.

"Objectivity," defined as the demonstrable exclusion of personal bias from scholarly accounts, becomes but another fantasy when read under the sign *interpretation*. Data are not passively obtained in what the French call the "human sciences." Rather, they are actively constructed in accordance with interpretive schemes implicit in scholarly questions posed.

For example, to ask "What is Man?" is to assume—much to the dismay of, say, Michel Foucault—that *Man* exists as a functional totality. That which is avowedly and undeniably "personal," therefore, makes its way into the investigative arena. Reader response criticism in recent years and postmodernist revisionary ratios have enabled the "creative critic" and the autobiographical theorist to produce what Elizabeth Bruss calls beautiful theories—unabashedly *personal* critiques.

My own turn toward a more personal voice has at least two sources—an emulation of black scholars attuned to the vernacular and a theoretical attraction to the enterprise in present-day expressive cultural investigation that privileges interpretation. There is also a third source. It is my determination to confront what I see as the dreadful academic "normalization" of such emergent fields as Afro-American and women's studies.

By normalization, I mean the imposition—by budget constraints, heightened conservative opinion, and benign neglect—of vaguely universalist goals. As corollaries to radical political activism—i.e., Black Power and women's liberation—black and women's studies are often held nowadays to require academic standardization if they are to endure.

The notion is that if black studies is *universalized* and *depoliticized* (withdrawn from clear social and political imperatives) it can become a hybridized concern for the "other" — a postmodernist forum, in other words, for a diverse body of "nontraditional" scholars. Similarly, despite a clear call to social activism, women's studies is urged to the study of "gender."

Though it is gratifying to witness the gravitation of unexpected scholars to such areas as black and women's studies, it is distressing to see black and women's studies beset by nonpoliticized and often dramatically uninformed readers. For the scholarship that the unexpected arrivants produce is motivated by ideals that are sometimes ironically akin to Platonic forms rather than ideas. That is to say, such scholars "cross over" because they have merely obtained "secondary" word that black and women's studies are areas productive of fresh insights.

Now when Greeks come bearing secondary intellectual gifts, it is time to have the steel helmets ready. For there is always a danger, as Langston Hughes put it, that Greeks will change one's song so that it doesn't sound like me anymore.

The sound that now resonates in my mind and that I deem of utmost value is not a universalist or expansionist (Greek) note. Rather, it is a personal, racially derived, and theoretically motivated chord. Its instrumental valley is the black vernacular.

The motives for such a sound include what can only be called a political determination to make progress. By comprehending the geographies of the black vernacular, I believe that I can move toward a correction and expansion of my earlier responses to, say, Toomer, Cullen, and the Harlem Renaissance. I can also, I believe, half-perceive and half-invent an area of Afro-American expressive spiritual depths where Toomer's and Cullen's collards and lieder are stewing in redolent harmony with the kale and bohemian aesthetics of Baraka, Neal, and Fuller.

If *anyone* feels, however, after reading the following essay, that the work is simply about departmental politics at my university, or merely concerned with "personal" matters, then he or she must secure gustatory advice and consume at least one helping of home-cooked greens before we try to talk further.

> In spite of myself . . . I find that I am actuated by a strong sense of race consciousness. This grows upon me, I find, as I grow older, and although I struggle against it, it colors my writing, I fear, in spite of everything I can do. There may have been many things in my life that have hurt me, and I find that the surest relief from these hurts is in writing.
>
> —Countee Cullen

> In the light of the current myth, in which art aims to become a "total experience," soliciting total attention, the strategies of impoverishment and reduction indicate the most exalted ambition art could adopt. Underneath what looks like a strenuous modesty, if not actual debility, is to be discerned an energetic secular blasphemy: the wish to attain the unfettered, unselective, total consciousness of "God."
>
> —Susan Sontag

> Art hurts. Art urges voyages—
> and it is easier to stay at home,
> the nice beer ready.
>
> —Gwendolyn Brooks

 Strategies, questions, and issues of "race" have been enormously influential, and troubling, in the creation and criticism of Afro-American literature and culture. Any black person in the United States who has aspired to the status of poet, singer, painter, or novelist has found him or herself confronted, automatically, by a tortuous psychosocial maze that begins with "race." One thinks, for example, of Phillis Wheatley bemoaning the fact that *only* Terence among Africans was enrolled in the poets' hall of fame:

> The happier *Terence* all the choir inspir'd,
> His soul replenish'd, and his bosom fir'd;
> But say, ye *Muses,* why this partial grace,
> To one alone of *Afric's* sable race;
> From age to age transmitting thus his name
> With the first glory in the rolls of fame?[1]

More contemporaneously, one recalls John A. Williams' haunting account *The Man Who Cried I Am*.[2] Under Western eyes, *Race* and *Art* have traditionally been considered dissociated signs, causing the creative person of clear racial designation, ambition, or allegiance to find him or herself pinioned on the horns of a specifically occidental dilemma. Surely black writers of the 1920s struggled in their own way with "race." This struggle can perhaps be equated with the ceaseless and mystical effluence of black folk wisdom: "there is a river."[3] The perpetual current of "race" in Afro-American life and letters is the subject of the present chapter, which constitutes an extension of my foregoing reflections on Countee Cullen and Jean Toomer — a meditative "update," as it were.

My update begins with a very recent event. The occasion was a meeting in the spring of 1986, devoted to "racial awareness." The meeting was called by the dean of the College of Arts and Sciences at the university where I teach. During the previous spring (1985), student protests surrounding a professor accused of racist pedagogy had resulted in commitments from various schools and colleges of my university to hold workshops and seminars on "racial awareness."

On the day of the dean's meeting, our Arts and Sciences committee gathered to seek a title for the lecture series we were proposing to increase racial awareness in our college. The signal fact about our search for a title was the reluctance of almost everyone to employ the word *race*. "Well," said the dean, "we could call it the 'Distinguished Black Scholars Series.'" A sigh of relief. "But," began another colleague, "we are not going to confine ourselves to black speakers, are we?" Consternation. Then I said, "I think we should call it 'The Dean's Lectures for Racial Awareness.' Why are we avoiding the word *race?*" "The Dean's Lectures on Race Relations" was the title chosen.

This personal anecdote succinctly captures, I believe, the turns that a white majority is capable of in the United States. Thirty years ago, the term "race" was affixed by whites to anything remotely related to "The Negro." In the 1960s, however, various "so-called" *races* accepted, endorsed, and, indeed, appropriated control of a domain that white culture had traditionally pointed to with an admixture of scorn, vindictiveness, morbid curiosity, and amusement. That domain was what might be called the racial quarter of America. From a sign of derogatory exclusion, "race" was unequivocally elevated during the sixties and seventies to a sign of proud exclusivity by people asserting their own supreme self-worth.

During black activist days of recent decades, for example, black Americans looked directly into the eyes of white cohorts and, paraphrasing the blues of Peetie Wheatstraw, said: "We are who we are: and all we was born to be!"[4] A *race* apart. Many blacks adamantly insisted on being left alone to develop what they believed was a sui generis *racial* tradition. Amiri Baraka's "I don't love you" — a poem that marked the poet's own departure from Greenwich Village — sounds the note of this stridently positive black acceptance of a racial imperative:

Whatever you've given me, whiteface glass
to look through, to find another there, another
what motherfucker? another bread tree mad at its
sacredness, and the law of some dingaling god,
    cold
as ice cucumbers, for the shouters and the
    wigglers,
and what was the world to the words of slick
    nigger fathers,
too depressed to explain why they could not
    appear to be men.

The bread fool. The don'ts of this white hell.
    The crashed eyes
of dead friends, standin at the bar, eyes
    focused on actual ugliness.

I don't love you. Who is to say what that will
    mean. I don't
love you, expressed the train, moves, and uptown
    days later
we look up and breathe much easier.

I don't love you[5]

To fully appreciate this manifesto of departure would require more space than the extant corpus of James Baldwin essays detailing the opponent, affective processes of black and white relationships in America. For the moment, it will suffice to say that "race," as an automatic label for derogation, virtually disappeared from black consciousness during the late 1960s. The sign became more generally a term of celebration than ever before.

There have, of course, always been RACE MEN and RACE WOMEN —Garveys and Bethunes urging, "Up you mighty race!"—in black American history. But before the sixties, the "mass-heart" of Afro-America had never so spiritedly accepted ethnic identification as a badge of honor. This mass acceptance meant the abrogation of traditional white definitions of "race" as the black masses set in motion a rite of inversion in which the former distinguisher ("race" as myth and sign of white superiority) became a mark of black glory.

Inspired by this radical rite of inversion, other interest groups in the United States took heart and worked similar inversions on "Indian," "Gay," "Woman," "Mexican American," "Puerto Rican," etc. When the semantic field of "race"—as the privileged American sign of *difference*—was shifted by blacks, the entire vocabulary (signifiers and signifieds) of relationship, kinship, and community in the United States was dramatically altered. Rather than a reactionary demarcation, that is to say, *race* became a revolutionary sign.

Screaming mobs of white mothers in New Orleans during that city's desegregation crises, white citizens' councils of Alabama and Georgia, and clans of Ku Kluxers everywhere were countered in our recent American past by a defiantly *racial* sound—a boisterous black voice declaiming: "We are Black, Beautiful. . . . and we *don't* love you!"

The effectiveness of rituals, however, lies in their contexts. Their utility as processes of demarcation inheres in their irreversibility. When a young person is read out of childhood or a woman is read into motherhood through prescribed rituals, neither can return to his or her preritual status. If the behaviors of black Americans vis-à-vis "race" during the sixties had been pure ritual, then their effects would have been *permanent,* irreversible. The pride, dignity, and elation assumed to accompany a new and distinctively racial status would have endured.

Unfortunately, the inversive rites of our recent past were merely components of a longstanding white American ritual. I mean, the ceaseless American ceremony of violence exemplified by exterminations of Indians, deportations and enslavement of Africans, imperialist warfare against inhabitants of the great Southwest. When America decided in recent years that it wanted "race" restored to old laws and ancient orders that sustained white hegemony, it simply sanctioned murder, suppression, and brutalization of blacks. (We *must* remember Attorney General John Mitchell's raids akin to Palmer's devastations of the left. We *must* recall J. Edgar Hoover as a man bound to violence.) The results of the brutal, illegal, and unconstitutional white restoration are indicated by statistical projections of our own era. We are told that when the 1990s arrive, the black family will be virtually extinct. The majority of black households will be headed by impoverished mothers and populated by children born out of wedlock to teenagers. Seventy percent of black males will be unemployed.[6]

"Law and Order" was the white American rallying cry for restoration. (We *must* remember a lawless president of the United States contorting his lawless face as he uttered those words.) Among the academically trained, the reassertion of traditional definitions and uses of *race* expressed itself as "pluralism" or, simply, AMERICAN, spelled with hearty capitals and uttered with the implicit understanding that the referent was a white male and identifiably Yankee "we." "Race," one might justifiably say, is today unquestionably in the hands once more of whites who would subject it to an academically sanctioned mystification — or eradicate it altogether in the name of a putatively benign empiricism.

In an engaging essay written almost a decade ago, the Afro-American critic Henry Louis Gates, Jr., claimed that I and others of the Black Aesthetic camp were proponents of what he designated "race and superstructure criticism."[7] In Gates's view, such criticism consisted of assiduous attempts by black critics to prove that Afro-American expressive products were *equal to* Western expressive modes. Compelled to battle derogatory judgments on *the race* and to assert racial equality, race and superstructure criticism, according to Gates, locked Black Aestheticians into a Western problematic. New and fruitful modes of cultural analysis could scarcely emerge from a myopic involvement with Western-controlled discourse.

If there was a flaw in past orientations of Afro-American criticism, however, it was not, as Gates suggests, one of emphasis, but one of direction. Afro-American criticism's emphasis on *race* has been entirely justified. But its critics have frequently made the mistake of looking away from, rather than directly to, their *own* racial vernacular in order to discover the powerful significance of *race* in the United States. They have often looked to Western discourse rather than to their own soulful valleys of sound. And it is, as I have already suggested, at the level of soul, cultural spirit work, or genius that one most effectively encounters sounds of the lowground that comprises a black cultural geography. It is at this level alone, for example, that the efforts of writers such as Jean Toomer and Countee Cullen can be effectively reexamined.

Where Cullen is concerned, we recognize an ambiguity of racial sentiment, an ambiguity considered "natural" by a liberal-humanist tradition. Like the familiar, generic "Negro" (the one who ever feels the "two-ness" referred to by W. E. B. DuBois' *The Souls of Black Folk*), Cullen felt the "two-ness" of his racial situation in the United States and reacted accordingly. He begged to be judged by "standard" criteria as "just a poet." Rather than be judged a racial "first," he wanted, somehow, to be adjudged by standards reserved for whitemale versifiers.

Rather than a failure of the imagination, one can view the Harlem Renaissance poet's desire as a unique inscription of the *racial* dynamics of Afro-American expressive culture. What one might fruitfully observe and analyze is the fact that Cullen came to realize through his work as a "Negro Poet" that there were certain inaudible facts, unspeakable realities, and whispered wisdoms that comprised a *necessary* awareness for a black person in the United States. The poet's realization—as for many thousands gone—hurt. His "Incident" and "Yet Do I Marvel" record this hurt, and, I believe, mark Cullen as a major *Afro-American* poet.

I would argue that to judge Cullen, in the face of such poems, by standards other than racial ones is to miss him altogether. Alan Shucard's recent critical biography entitled *Countee Cullen* demonstrates, I believe, how the poet can be so misconstrued.[8] Shucard states his determination to render a no-frills account of the Harlem Renaissance poet's life and career. He tells us in his preface that in order to be true to scholarly ideals he had to separate "the demands of conscience" from "those of the heart." Cullen is, thus, viewed as a poet of limited black success, one who "streaked" across the literary scene in the 1920s and quickly descended. Shucard defines him as a poet whose best volume was *Color.*

Two purposes are served by the type of reading Shucard offers. First, it redeems Cullen from the charge of being a traitor to "race." If *Color* is the single most important contribution, then Cullen never escaped a racial province. Such a reading, however, confines Cullen's critical reputation to a single volume.

While it is certainly true that Shucard does not confine his Twayne publication to a discussion of *Color,* it is also true that the biographer seems to have settled on his conclusions in advance of an adequately imaginative reading of the poet's corpus. Why, for example, if the most valuable work is indisputably Cullen's first volume, did the poet continue to write, to think of himself as a creative artist, and to venture into fields such as the novel and the drama after *Color?* And why do readers (especially Afro-American readers) continue to think of Cullen in terms far grander than those proposed by Shucard?

Shucard does not, I think, deliberately shirk such inquiries. His *objective* orientation (conscience, and not heart, in the lead) simply forecloses the possibility of his hearing the almost inaudible levels of Afro-American discourse that mark a distinctive black poetic experience in America and that forestall Cullen's appearing before us today as a "failed" writer. Shucard writes:

> It should not be taken as axiomatic that it [Cullen's poetry] can even be called "black," though it was composed by a black man, for Cullen himself denied that there is such a literary phenomenon as "black poetry." In a limited sense, he was correct: after all, black American poets are American; use, except for dialect poems,

general American English; and heed the same urge to create as their white counterparts—are bound to the same muse, even if they might argue against white Attic origins. (P. 13)

One wonders, on reading this observation, whether Shucard, who seems to deny the very existence of a uniquely black poetic tradition, has perused Stephen Henderson's *Understanding the New Black Poetry* or even casually surveyed Eugene Redmond's *Drumvoices*. Cullen's biographer seems to neglect altogether the force of recent Afro-American criticism and theory, relying exclusively on traditional New Critical procedures for his analysis and conclusions.

If, however, Shucard had turned to a discursive history of Afro-America, he would surely have realized that in black America there is indeed a sui generis field of speaking.[9] One *can* argue, of course, that the intended audience for such a field should be a "disinterested" and universal one. But the black southern masses streaming into the North at the turn of the century did not, it would appear, endorse or mandate such universality. Dislocated language and intellectual and emotional complexes in an instant of time— designed, as these poetic features are now considered to be, for *universal* response—were not what they required. Rather, the masses came in search of economic betterment and sure signs that a better *racial* day would follow from their daring and optimistic change of place.

The work of Countee Cullen, which sounded like poetry was supposed to sound and which received marvelous kudos from white critics and readers alike, offered a sign that a black minister's son could sure show white people a thing or two about taking a northern world of *changed place* by storm. Rather than special pleading on behalf of Cullen's oeuvre—in defense or apology, as it were, for his poetic strategies and output—my interpretation is a contextualization. An understanding of the demands of the 1920s helps, I believe, to clarify the poet's bitter disappointment when his own choice of expressive strategies failed to carry the day for him—or for *the race*.

Who can doubt, finally, that Cullen, who grew up in and served the black Harlem community throughout his life, sang many a deep-night blues as he pondered fundamental regions and reasons of blackness in America? If he is attractive to us, as a man who desired to be judged as "just a poet," it is because his desire encapsulates every Afro-American's *dream,* or fantasy, of a world where race, as a sign of derogation, would be refigured. Like all Afro-Americans, however, Cullen inhabited a world where race *was* a derogatory sign and where the only place that such a sign could be refigured was in racial memory—the valleys, as it were, ringing with black song and soundings. Cullen, thus, becomes a veritable sign of struggle, a poet *malgré lui,* encoding inaudible reaches of the low and common valley of *blackness.* His ironic confessionals, rewritings of the old legacies of color, and invocations of Afro-American religious testimonial forms bespeak his downward journey toward a place that *hurts,* but also heals. Such a descent is not, I believe, apprehensible in New Critical or "nonracial" critical terms.

One way of explaining what an Afro-American spokesperson accomplishes when he or she is most distinctively "racial" is to say that at such moments his or her work constitutes not only a descent but a *breakthrough.* The result of a breakthrough is not easily comprehended by familiar, objective modes of criticism. For it is more likely to take form as the agonizing moments of Cullen, or the whole of Jean Toomer's *Cane,* than, say, a finished ode of the Keatsian variety that Cullen adored. The breakthrough has only one clear categorical identification: it is distinctively *racial.* Beyond this, it defies familiar taxonomies.

What is *Cane?* What school of "general American" poetry describes Cullen? The products of Afro-American expressive culture are, frequently, stuttered, polyphonic, dissociative—fragmented, ambivalent, or incomplete. They "urge voyages" and require inventive, personal response.

The preacher who expects satisfactorily to read a formal, *written* homily to his congregation is not a *black* or a *racial* preacher. For the black preacher knows, as the title of a recent scholarly monograph states: "I've Got the Word in Me and I Can Sing It, You Know!"[10] The black preacher breaks through often even into a vernacular song that says: "I've walked in valleys where I couldn't hear *nobody* pray."[11] Such an example from the black vernacular suggests that *race* carries distinctive expressive cultural incumbencies.

Rather than read Jean Toomer as an exception to a black expressive rule, or as an exotic, one can view him in the wonderfully sane way provided by his best biographer, Professor Nellie McKay.[12] McKay defines Toomer as a representative moment in the larger dialectic of race in the United States. She identifies the black writer's life as a search for wholeness, for a total integration of his own personality, and an attempt to unify mankind by means of a higher spirituality. Toomer, in brief, is identified as a black mystic who sought a breakthrough and found it most decisively in the valleys and lowgrounds of Blackness.[13]

Cane, then, if it is read in fitting terms, offers a record and model of the breakthrough as I have defined it.[14] The implicit goal of the agonized consciousness that informs Toomer's book — serving variously as narrator of short stories, persona of poems, and protagonist of drama — is to capture the sound of a racial soul and convert it into an expressive product equivalent in beauty and force to Afro-American folk songs, or ecstatic religious performances.

Talk of "soul" in *Cane* commences with the protagonist of "Karintha," whose soul was ripened too soon. In "Song of the Son," the speaker describes his task as catching "thy plaintive soul, leaving soon gone." The "soul" in question is that of "slavery" — a quintessential Afro-American state — and the speaker's self-assigned task is to turn the sound of this state into "An everlasting song, a singing tree." The poem that follows "Song of the Son" in *Cane* is "Georgia Dusk" where we find southern black singers invested with an African spirit — a "genius," as I have noted earlier, for "making folk-songs from soul sounds." "Soul," thus, seems to be a principal focus of *Cane*'s energies.

"Calling Jesus" speaks of the unincorporated "soul" in need of a covering messiah, and Ralph Kabnis defines the drama of his situation in terms of the violence, terror, beauty, sin, spirituality, discourse, and prophecy that affect his peculiar *soul.* "Soul" ceaselessly appears as the sign of a numinous, racial domain of experience that can be reached only through dissociation, through *descent.* I think the descent or breakthrough required is, finally, allied to the more familiar category *trance.*

Trance is a sleep or dreamlike state characterized by ego excursus (sometimes called a "dissolving" of personality) and loss of sensory and motor contact with physical surroundings.[15] It can be induced by schizophrenia, hypnosis, hysteria, shamanistic rituals, possession, psychoactive drugs, or half-willed, half-possessed mediumistic circumstances. The mediumistic mode is the one most apparent in *Cane*.

In mediumistic trance, the medium is possessed by a benign spirit that transmits socially beneficial prophecy, advice, knowledge, healing, and precognition. Instead of the glossolalia or kinesthetic moments of possession trances, mediumistic trances produce intelligible words and conclude with a degree of memorability.

In all trances, psychic phenomena occur that defy empirical law and scientific explanation — fire walking, healing, deeds of uncanny strength or knowledge. "To *trance*," as an active behavior, is to make contact with the numinous element of the universe, and in *Cane* that element is coded as the history of the Afro-American *soul* in its tortuous striving to convert a *possessed* state of slavery into the liberated beauty of a freeing and, I think, deeply Afro-American religious song.

Why *trance?* Consider Fern's ecstatic moment in the canefield (where "time" and "space" have no meaning). Think of Barlo in the story "Esther":

> A clean-muscled, magnificent, black-skinned Negro, whom she had heard her father mention as King Barlo, suddenly drops to his knees on a spot called the SPITOON. . . . His smooth black face begins to glisten and to shine. Soon, people notice him, and gather round. His eyes are rapturous *upon* the heavens, lips and nostrils quiver. Barlo is in a religious trance. (P. 20)

Think of Dan Moore, in total dissociation from a theater's audience, following the bloodlines of a black heritage to the low underground. (Can't one say that the very "king" in "Esther" is a "low bar" as in Caribbean limbo, where one must "get down" if he would survive a *dread* marginality?) We have John's trance in "Theater," Paul's epiphanic dissociation in "Bona and Paul." Both Father John and Ralph Kabnis dissociate from their surroundings and utter words like Barlo's — words that have been whispered "deep down" in their ears during trance. Of Kabnis: "Half-way to the old man, he falls and lies quite still. Perhaps an hour passes" (p. 112). Father John has been many years in a trance: "To the left, sitting in a high-backed chair which stands upon a low platform, the old man. He is like a bust in black walnut. Gray-bearded. Gray-haired. Prophetic. Immobile" (p. 104).

The physical immobility of *Cane*'s entranced mediums stands in juxtaposition with their psychic dynamism. Toomer's mediums are channels of passage, agencies of spirit transmission. They serve also as interactive forces ensuring communication with benign ancestral spirits. Such mediums are agents and agencies, in a word, of the *breakthrough*. The gifts of their various descents are prophecy and advice — salvific wisdom.

Further, the behavior of *Cane*'s mediums — their ecstatic, dissociative speaking which is forcefully and beautifully exceptional and discontinuous with everyday life — can move a community to contagion behavior. "This much is certain: an inspired negress, of wide reputation for being sanctified, drew a portrait of a black madonna on the courthouse wall," as a function of Barlo's trance.

And if a community is infected and affected by trance, then a medium's behavior can, paradoxically, be defined as "normal." Of the town's reaction to Barlo: "Soon, people notice him, and gather round. . . . Barlo is in a religious trance. *Town folks know it. They are not startled. They are not afraid*" (my emphasis, p. 20).

Margaret Mead and Gregory Bateson, as well as Jane Belo, have provided captivating anthropological accounts of the "normalcy" of trance in Balinese culture.[16] These anthropologists suggest that an overreliance on Western, empirical resources for viewing life may impel us to label trance "aberrant," when, in fact, it is a psychically powerful and efficacious *norm* in cultures less moved by science than, say, the United States.

In *Cane,* the ancestral spirit of a race is designated by the term *soul.* Mediumistic contact with this soul is almost always coded in terms drawn from a Judeo-Christian tradition. The spirit "voice" that Barlo hears is Jesus'. Fern, in a hysterical trance, sings a religious song. Dan Moore "returns" from his entranced meditation on racial bloodlines with a message about Jesus as a leper.

And Father John and Kabnis interact with only the briefest array of signs as their middle ground — "soul," "sin," "Jesus," "death," and "the Bible."

I think that the mediumistic conflation of "soul" and "Jesus" ("Calling Jesus" offers a primary example) in *Cane* results from the awareness achieved by the work's informing consciousness that the lowground survival, endurance, and growth of a race of Africans in America are functions of a spirituality that most clearly manifests itself in black religious discourse, song, and ritual performance. *Cane* moves, at least in part, under the influence of Afro-American religious ecstasy conceived of as a "language" of the *soul* of a race. This "soul language" or "soul sound" is deemed an appropriate — if laconic, torturous, frenzied, and fragmented — expressive vehicle for sounding the depths of a people.

There are any number of features of Toomer's work that attest the discursive and performative influences of Afro-American religion. The appearance of visionary and ecstatic trance is only the broadest of such features. For there is also a continuous employment by the work's informing consciousness of the call-and-response pattern of text-and-interjection familiar to Afro-American preachers and their Amen Corners. Think of the pines "whispering" to Jesus in "Becky": "O pines, whisper to Jesus; tell Him to come and press sweet Jesus-lips against their lips and eyes." Or, consider the contrapuntal interjections in "Carma" such as "Hi! Yip! God has left the Moses-people for the nigger."

Such interjections *play,* as it were, against *Cane*'s narrative, producing a rhythm akin to Afro-American call-and-response. "Rhobert" contains the response "Brother, life is water that is being drawn off"; "Theater" contains the rhythmic "O dance! O dance!" Such textual "amens" are lowground testimonials to soulful energy.

The interjections that play within *Cane*'s texture are, in essence, sounds of desire. They capture an almost mystical longing for something that in "Fern" is "called God" or that is described in "Esther" (implicitly through the protagonist's desire to be a "black madonna") as a new birth, a "dawnin of the mornin light."

The sounds are objective correlatives, soul (or sole) *sounds,* for the frenzied spiritual *apprehension* of the beauty and mystery of inaudible valleys. The almost ironic assignment of tangible sound to states of black desire reads as follows in "Avey": "The [locomotive] engines of this valley have a whistle, the echoes of which sound like iterated gasps and sobs. I always think of them as crude music from the soul of Avey" (p. 44). While Barlo preaches a more or less straightforward and visionary sermon on his "return" from entrancement, most of *Cane*'s characters, speakers, personas, and interjected narrational choruses are akin to ecstatic shouters of the black church. Seized by the spirit's frenzy—designated, I think, in *Cane* as Jesus' messianic presence—these speakers attempt to bring up from the low valleys sounds (talk) that will create a new day. The goal of ecstatic and mediumistic trance in *Cane* is a *Vision Splendid*—akin to that of black religion—which will convert the wisdom of an ancestral and ancestrally religious spirit into a humane and harmonious world.

The conversion of *soul sounds*—making their way to a community of hearers through a sensitive medium—into *folk song* is not deemed a reactive gesture in *Cane*. Rather, the transformative spiritual and expressive process seems a defining strategy of the book's writing of *race*. Mystical longings, a desire to transcend empirical boundaries and material limitations are sounded by *Cane* as the entrancing essence of Afro-America.

What are sometimes taken as flaws of *Cane*—for example, its truncated character development and mysterious associative phrases—are fully comprehensible to the reader who grasps the significance of trance. For the informing consciousness of the book strives to unite itself with the spiritual/emotional/sounding network that comprises the lowground of black experience. And the report of this consciousness (because it is a report of the ineffable) has a laconic, skeletal, and often mysterious character.

A consideration of *Cane* under the sign of "trance" contradicts, of course, a reading of the work as anything resembling a journey toward what is traditionally defined as "art." Toomer's text bears little resemblance, for example, to the linear representations that characterize realism, social realism, or the *novel*. From the perspective of trance—with all of the Afro-American religious implications suggested by my foregoing discussion—Cane is less an artwork than a product of what Susan Sontag designates an "aesthetics of silence."[17]

By the phrase, Sontag means a "modern" theory and practice that seek release from, rather than representation of and communication with, human consciousness. The artist aspires to overcome the duplicity and historicity of language, to break free of "everyday experience" and the criteria of a conventional ART. His or her goal becomes the ecstatic, mystical zones of the spirit. Dissociation and a trancelike "memorability" are normal for such an aesthetics:

> In the early, linear version of art's relation to consciousness, a struggle was discerned between the "spiritual" integrity of the creative impulses and the distracting "materiality" of ordinary life, which throws up so many obstacles in the path of authentic sublimation. But the newer version, in which art is part of a dialectical transaction with consciousness, poses a deeper, more frustrating conflict. The "spirit" seeking embodiment in art clashes with the "material" character of art itself. Art is unmasked as gratuitous, and the very concreteness of the artist's tools (and, particularly in the case of language, their historicity) appears as a trap. Practiced in a world furnished with secondhand perceptions, and specially confounded by the treachery of words, the artist's activity is cursed with mediacy. Art becomes the enemy of the artist, for it denies him the realization—the transcendence—he desires. (P. 182)

Surely Toomer's work is infused with what we can call a religious, mystical, or entranced force antagonistic to "art" in the same way that an "aesthetics of silence" refigures a traditional expressivity. Though Kabnis defines himself as a man of "words," he also realizes, to his own desperate astonishment, that the "ugly" thing (objectified by murderous lynchers) that is polluting his soul is *fed by* words. Merely arranged in a traditional Christian problematic of "sin," "Jesus," "death," and "the Bible," words are ineffectual. Only when they enter into entranced performance, it would seem, do they give birth to sounds of a new order. It is only then that speech by a mystical transcendence passes into union with (for want of a better term) "Jesus." Jesus becomes a salvific spirit who takes his contours not from the words of a book (the Bible) but from the sounds of cotton and cane fields, whispering pines, "underground" locomotives, and urban trolleys. These quotidian sounds of black everyday life become a people's entrancing song.

During his brief sojourn in Georgia in the early 1920s, Toomer underwent an entrancing experience of an Afro-American "aesthetics of silence." In "Kabnis," an ecstatic black religious service is the signifying background ritual for Layman and Halsey's tales of bizarre white lynching rituals. The shrieks and frenzy of the church unnerve Kabnis, causing him to lash out at the materialism and duplicity of black preachers. But the informing consciousness of *Cane* captures, in this penultimate moment, a vision of strategies that lead Afro-Americans beyond a brutal, everyday cacophony to a whispered wisdom of the numinous. Entrancing performance moves the race beyond sinful and murderous death to the "birth song" that concludes "Kabnis."

I believe that the difference between what Sontag describes as an aesthetics of silence and the lowground cultural soundings that I have attempted to describe is that black performances are not self-willed processes engaged by an individual "artist" or, better, "anti-artist." The black valley is communal space where the medium's work is abortive without contagious group response. The trance, in a word, is dependent upon folk sounds for its very inducement. There is a reciprocity, then, in which "soul sounds" that hint of a racial "genius" surpassing speech lead to the medium's entrancement. Trance produces, in turn, further sounds or songs that are, at best, metonyms for the deepest spiritual reaches of inaudible valleys.

A further characterization of states of entrancement in *Cane* might be the phrase "mystical states of being." For example, Fern is clearly a spiritual figure who has attained union with the holy; her vision (eyes) literally flows with something that the narrator calls "God." The sound with which she is associated is that of a Jewish cantor. Further, she has given up—in the manner of the medieval anchoress—the pleasures of the body, spending her days in trance-like solitariness, hating the world, and sharing symbolically in

Christ's passion by turning just slightly aside from the post nail that she refuses to remove.

Elsewhere in *Cane,* we find Father John entombed in the manner of the anchorite, given over to trancelike contemplations of Jesus, sin, and death.

A mystical bent also reveals itself in the book's representations of an impulse to articulate a form of discourse, a "talk" that will "push back the fringes of pines on new horizons." I believe what is implicit in the "talk" of *Cane* — as in leaves swaying "rusty with talk" and the soft pines whispering — is the impulse and intention to *pray.* Through prayer one reaches the face of God — achieves a sense of His ineffable being.

Toomer's talking males are, it is true, impotent in the everyday world because they, like medieval mystics, are compulsively moved beyond the world, seeking through their prayerful talk to express the lowgrounds of black spirituality. The bizarre reports and seemingly abnormal behaviors on their return from trance to the world (think of Dan Moore's words of Jesus, or Paul's utterances to the doorman at the Crimson Gardens) are earnest — if tortured — attempts to capture the ineffable. Think: if God, or black soul force, were amenable to words or easily describable, they would not be God, or *soul.* There can be no "art" of the breakthrough. Perhaps only its *performance* can occur. The mystical experience is by its very nature antithetical to normal representation — artistic or otherwise. It demands (if that vast body of black-church testimonials can be credited) its own special vocabulary and sounding rhythms — a grammar, as it were, of the black valley that will "carry it along." From "Song of the Son":

> Pour O pour that parting soul in song.
> O pour it in the sawdust glow of night,
> Into the velvet pine-smoke air to-night,
> And let the valley carry it along.
> And let the valley carry it along.

I want to suggest that Toomer did not bring the techniques of modern "art" to bear on Afro-American experience. Rather, he found himself possessed — entranced — by the soul sounds and folk songs of Georgia's dusky valleys. He discovered, on low ancestral ground, a spirituality and sounding communal performance that outstripped any mere artistic desire. While he may have brought with him to Sparta, Georgia, the yearnings of the modern artist, he departed as an Afro-American medium.

In a sense, Georgia's Afro-American expressive rituals compelled Toomer to abandon art in favor of a black aesthetics of silence. The expressive mode that possessed him does not lead to dreams of creative products that pander to exotic American tastes or that seek conformity with the standard. Toomer did not desire, upon leaving the South, a personal corpus of "black books." Instead, he desired mystical union. He left Georgia determined to achieve a sounding of the world that would convert desire and silence into an AMERICAN song. Which is simply to say that he was in possession of a black humaneness, communality, and spirit force that have always been, in Lance Jeffers' wonderful phrase, "more American than America."[18]

Only by paying special attention to the sociology, psychology, and entrancing sounding of *race* does a critic of Afro-American culture arrive at an inclusive perspective. While one of the impulses of the late 1980s seems to be the abandonment of even the word *race,* I find myself, perhaps not unlike Cullen, insensibly drawn to its resounding rituals.

Somehow, I cannot persuade myself that a black person in America, or South Africa, or the Caribbean, or anywhere else in today's world is anything other than a *black* person—a person preeminently and indisputably governed, in his life choices and expectations, by a long-standing and pervasive discourse called *race.*

What seems well advised to me, therefore, is the construction of analytical models for Afro-American expressive culture that allow us to hear its racial resonances. What is needed, I believe, is a "criticism of silence" to match the depths of a magnificently entrancing black sounding of experience. The emergence of such a criticism will surely constitute one step toward a fuller comprehension of Afro-American spirit work.

I trust that my engagement with such a project in the foregoing

discussion brings a fuller resonance to our hearing of Countee
Cullen and Jean Toomer. In a very real sense, it seems to me that
Cullen, a minister's gentle son, and Toomer, a mystic in process,
both tacitly endorsed poetic promises of the breakthrough like
those resonant in the Caribbean writer Derek Walcott's assertion:
"I have never separated the writing of poetry from prayer. I have
grown up believing it is a vocation, a religious vocation."[19] A
"vocation," or *work* of the racial spirit, is surely a fitting designation for the labors of Toomer and Cullen as well as a fit naming
of the critical enterprise that must be brought to bear on their
work if we would truly hear.

 IV

"These Are Songs If You Have the / Music": An Essay on Imamu Baraka

I discovered LeRoi Jones during my first year of graduate school (1965–66). His second volume of poetry, *The Dead Lecturer,* with its brooding cover portrait, became a source of pleasure. I read and reread the poems and felt sad or enraged or envious, seeking to make sense of arcane imagery and delighting in a black persona's suave hipness. Addison Gayle, a classmate of mine, was amused by my "discovery." He had known Jones personally in New York. He felt the poet had "come a long way" since *The Dead Lecturer.* He had departed the "beat" life and existential angst of Greenwich Village and established the Harlem Black Arts Repertory Theatre School, an institution that Gayle had known firsthand.

But what, precisely, did it mean to "come a long way"? I remember musing in the California sunshine of UCLA about a brownstone in Harlem, and hordes of people marching in and out of a "Theatre School." Inside, I envisioned university classrooms and performance spaces and busy instructors and students. Jones I pictured in the *Dead Lecturer* mode, but dressed as a college president. The high intellectual overseer. My musings scarcely accorded, as I shall later make clear, with the realities of Jones's Black Arts enterprise.

In the 1960s, a type of *Code Napoléon* surrounded the Black Arts. Biography — or where you came from — was far less important than where you were "coming from." Dashikis and Afros made nonbourgeois black folks of us all. Hence my perception of Jones was not of a man who had already walked several roads and still had many more to walk. I took him at his own self-definition; in my eyes, he was a spiritual leader (Imamu). I was not uncritical; I recognized genius when I saw it. I simply was not critical enough.

I followed the Imamu's various name changes through the early seventies, witnessed his shifting allegiances, and poured over verse in *Black Magic,* essays in *Home,* and the punchy black revolutionary plays. For me, they were all Black Aesthetic scripture. Nobody, in my estimation, was as good as LeRoi Jones/Imamu Amiri Baraka.

The shift that Baraka made away from cultural nationalism in the mid-seventies was inexplicable to me. How could the Imamu abandon a cause that he had both half-invented and brilliantly and stridently propounded? (Remember, the *code* prevented my knowing the biography in any of its difficult details.) I was especially troubled by Baraka's desertion because Hoyt Fuller was distressed. I really did not feel ideologically betrayed in my own right. Fuller conveyed to me his profound regret about Baraka's departure, seeing it as a crippling fragmentation of a community that had just come into formation. "But," said Hoyt, "I've known him and the others who want to be Marxists for a long time. They are intelligent men who have to do what they think is right."

I wrote the essay that follows when Baraka was considered an "other," a strange amphibian swimming in Marxist waters. The essay was extrapolated from a larger work, never published, entitled "Beyond the Serpent's Fold," which I wrote for Brown University's Rites and Reason project.

I knew when I wrote the reflections that follow that Baraka was one of the most engaging subjects I had ever encountered, and the resultant essay is still one of my favorites. Its subject was, in fact, a kind of intellectual hero for me. And even in the face of such facts as his abandonment of not only the beatnik poets of Greenwich Village but also his wife and children, I stubbornly

refused to acknowledge that there could be questions about his
wholeness, or integrity. What could have been more American?
Baraka himself has perpetually displayed the same kind of heroic
faith. A peculiar and paradoxical space for heroes has unceas-
ingly marked his life and work. For me, in 1976, he remained the
man who had energetically begun a Black Arts movement and
written verse that would have tested the skill of Brooks and
Warren. He was also a courageous man who had issued stern
repudiations — in the vernacular — of a white creative and critical
enterprise: "We want a black poem. And a / Black World." He
did much to bring about both the poem and the world that many
of us believed in fervently during the days of the Black Aesthetic.
What preeminently his career — in the years that I analyze in the
following essay — manifests is, I believe, a version of that ceaseless movement of an Afro-American expressive cultural spirit that
as easily changes its name or face as its place of performance.

Surely what was driving Baraka in his moments of greatest
commitment and integrity was an impulse to pray — to be a
medium of the spirit. At the close of his foreword to the anthology *Black Fire,* coedited with Larry Neal, he pronounces: "We
[who are included in the anthology] are presenting. Your various
selves. We are presenting, from God, a tone, your own. Go on.
Now."

A religious spirit from both God and the depths of a distinctive ("Your own") soul arises as the numinous discourse of a
black cultural self-in-motion. It seems to me that a LeRoi Jones
who found himself — like Countee Cullen — insensibly drawn
toward models of racial expression and, like Jean Toomer, longing
for the mystical face of God suggests, at least, the prospective
continuities available under the sign of Afro-American spirit
work.

 The Alabama night settled on a small shack at the edge
of Selma. Sitting by a fire, made hastily to keep off the
chill, a young civil rights worker recalled a "hot, late
summer day" in Wilcox County.[1] Surrounded by deputies, lines
of black people were waiting to vote. Suddenly:

A white man leaped from the rank of deputies into the midst of
the students. Fists clenched in the air, he shook a writhing, green
snake. . . . The man tried to force the snake into a boy's mouth.
When the youngster gritted his teeth and pursed his lips, the man
laughed and tried to stuff his sickness down other throats. . . .
When, desperately, a victim threw out an arm to protect himself,
knocking the snake to the street, the man grew wide-eyed with
shock and indignation. Two of the deputies came dashing forward.
They led the Negro to a squad car. At the stationhouse, Sheriff
Jim Clark's deputies charged him with assault and jailed him.[2]

The black man's jailing is less striking than his physical reaction
to the white man's "sickness." The intensity of that hot southern
moment — with its image of blacks passively waiting, unprotected
by the laws of the region — lies in the sudden rising of the black
man's arm. Amazed, perhaps terrified, the white law moves into
action. The frame might be frozen as a pointed comment on the
1960s.

During the decade, blacks moved decisively away from the
Christian humility and Gandhian forbearance that marked the
strategy of Martin Luther King. And as their voices became more
strident, their actions more daringly aggressive, the police forces
of America were converted from domestic law enforcement agencies into what seemed heavily armed military regiments. It was
not blacks alone for whom these forces were upgraded. Young
whites also became vociferous and aggressive as America's involvement in Vietnam increased. By the fall of 1963, it was clear to
many that the optimistic mood of the fifties had been replaced
by one of violence and despair. In that year, Medgar Evers, John
F. Kennedy, and four young, black, Birmingham, Alabama, Sunday school worshipers were murdered. The violence of their deaths
was not singular; it was simply the most publicly lamented. Com-
bining with it — in the North and South alike — was an outgoing
hostility that threatened to destroy the nation. The Johnson ad-
ministration's passage of the Civil Rights Bill of 1964 and its
launching of a "War on Poverty" served to channel some of the
restless energies of the liberation struggle. But by 1966 both blacks
and whites knew that America was destined for extremes. Stokeley
Carmichael, president of the Student Nonviolent Coordinating

Committee, urged blacks to substitute "Black Power" for civil rights in their demands. And in many of those urban concentrations of blacks in the North and West he was heeded. The new phrase rang out with the sound of gunfire and the rumble of tanks that characterized ghetto uprisings. In 1968, Huey Newton and Bobby Seale, two young black men from Oakland, California, heightened the conflict, which had already reached near hysterical proportions with the assassination of Martin Luther King on April 4.

Newton and Seale organized the Black Panther Party for Defense and Justice as a group whose avowed intentions included the bearing of arms and the destruction of the white world's power over the black inner city. Cries for Black Power changed to fierce calls for Black Revolution. On college campuses, young blacks adopted the posture and rhetoric of revolt and moved to close down these institutions if their demands for black studies programs, increased black enrollment, and more black faculty were not met. Meanwhile, black communities continued to erupt in civil disorder, and thousands of young war protestors were clubbed into retreat during the Democratic convention in the summer of 1968. Later that year, Richard Nixon came to power with the rallying cry "Law and Order."

The last two years of the decade and the beginning of the 1970s found black men and women throughout America with their arms raised in the closed-fist salute of Black Power — Black Revolution. Many had more than fists to clench; they had sophisticated weapons. But their picking up the gun did little good. The Black Panthers, and virtually every other American radical group, were effectively eliminated by a government-sanctioned wave of repression that might be equated with the violence directed at organized labor earlier in this century. When the Vietnamese war drew to an agonizing conclusion, talk of the imminent overthrow of white America had waned. Those symbols of the proposed Black Nation — the Afro hair style, the dashiki, the tricolored flag — had begun to disappear. Soon, the country at large had to contend with the despair of Watergate.

The nature of black people's actions during the 1960s and early 1970s, however, left them more cause for pride than despair. Their arms had been raised in a gesture of unconditional refusal, and many had granted their allegiance to the black nationalist doctrines so convincingly advocated by a man like Malcolm X. It was paradoxical, of course, that those who had so recently come into contact with the written history of the West felt compelled to reject it. It was as though possession of what Richard Wright called "a vocabulary of history" gave blacks precisely the terms they needed to protect themselves, to knock the serpent into the street. Or, to place the matter in another light, it was as though black people had arrived at the Western city only to find it stricken with plague or caught in the bright flames of its destruction.

As an alternative to the sickness and death at hand, they proposed a new nation founded on those distinctively black and African elements that had never been allowed within the boundaries of the city. Rather than study the tortuous coils of the dying, they sought to bring forth new life. Black writers were in the forefront of this effort. And no canon reflects the process more accurately than that of Imamu Amiri Baraka (né LeRoi Jones).

Amiri Baraka

Baraka began writing as what he calls a "schwartze Bohemian."
The mode is caricatured in *Preface to a Twenty-Volume Suicide
Note* (1961):[3]

> They laught,
> and religion was something
> he fount in coffee shops, by God
> It's not that I got enything
> against cotton, nosiree, by God
> It's just that . . .
>> Man lookatthatblonde
>> whewee!
>
> (P. 10)

The early poetry is sometimes a verse of "maudlin nostalgia / that
comes on / like terrible thoughts about death" (p. 17). At other
moments, it approximates a game of surreal self-display like that
of the speaker in "Scenario IV":

> The motion of the mind! Smooth; I jiggle & clack stomping one
> foot & the clothesline swings. Fabulie Verwachsenes. Ripping this
> one off in a series of dramatic half-turns I learned many years ago
> in the orient, Baluba: "The power to cloud men's minds" etc., which
> I'm sure you must have heard about, doodle-doo. & then I'm sitting
> in this red chair, humming, feet still pecking at the marble floor. . .
> (Pp. 22–23)

Its prevailing tone is one of elegant despair tempered by an
inclination for the grotesque and the absurd.

There are instances, however, when the poet brings clear focus
to what he describes as the "Mosaic of disorder I own" (p. 27).
In the following lines, for example, he sets forth images that are
central to his canon:

> Emotion. Words.
> Waste, No clear delight.
> No light under my fingers. The room, The
> walls, silent & deadly. Not
> Music.
>
> (P. 32)

This is a rendering of the sealed consciousness, the mind in its silences and the body bereft of touch. The "room" appears time and again in Baraka's poetry. Its structures—walls and windows—may be set by the sea or on the wet grounds of a landscape that overlooks the waters. The person occupying the room joins a company characterized as "Isolate / Land creatures in a wet unfriendly world" (p. 18). But even though the poet feels cut off in his distances where "Not even cars . . . are real" (p. 38) and he is "barely human" (p. 35), he is still capable of sharp insights that bring an understanding of his own and society's plight. His makeup as an artist is not entirely solipsistic:

> What are
> influences?
> A green truck
> wet & glowing, seance
> of ourselves, elegy for the sea
> at night, my flesh
> a woman's. At the fingertips
> soft white increased coolness
> from the dark
> sea
>
> (P. 36)

The sea of everyday existence—including the mundane sight of a truck or the love of a woman—invades and shapes the room's spaces. Moreover, the poet realizes that what keeps him from turning outward to the world of flesh and influences is a kind of Western enervation:

> No use for beauty
> collapsed. with moldy breath
> done in. Insidious weight
> of cankered dreams. Tiresias'
> weathered cock
>
> (Pp. 24–25)

There are at least two adequate readings for the title of the poem in which these lines appear: "Way Out West." One reading of "way out" implies a distant locale, while another signifies a "way out" or bizarre territory. Caught in his hermetic room, the poet can still critique the outside environment and recognize his need for a broader range. His despair, in any case, may derive from a definition of writing that sees the poem as

A
turning away
from what
it was
had moved
us
A
madness

(P. 40)

Clearly, influences would be irrelevant to a canon conforming perfectly to such a view. Furthermore, the individual poem might be reduced to the experience of "the spent lover / smelling his fingers" (p. 41). In a sense, the definition itself and the fact that "nothing is happening to me (in this world)" (p. 27) are conditions of what the poet considers his own inescapable Americanness:

African blues
does not know me. Their steps, in sands
of their own
land. A country
in black & white, newspapers
blown down pavements
of the world Does
not feel
what I am
. . . Africa
is a foreign place. You are
as any other sad man here
american.

(P. 47)

The lines are from "Notes for a Speech," the final poem in *Preface*. They seem to promise little success for the poet who says:

I am thinking
of a dance. One I could
invent, if there
were music. . .

(P. 32)

The jaded world of *Preface,* with its bare glimmerings of hope,
is an impressionistic reflection of the external reality Baraka found
himself involved with in the early 1960s. He says in "Cuba Libre,"
a 1960 essay from *Home* (1965):[4]

> The most severe condemnation of American leaders by the Ameri-
> can intellectual is that they are "bumblers," unintelligent but well-
> meaning clowns. But we do not realize how much of the horrible
> residue of these paid liars is left in our heads. . . . We reject the
> blatant, less dangerous lie, in favor of the subtle subliminal lie,
> which is more dangerous because we feel we are taking an intelligent
> stance, not being had. . . . There is a certain hopelessness about
> our attitude that can even be condoned. The environment sickens.
> The young intellectual living in the United States inhabits an ugly
> void. He cannot use what is around him, neither can he revolt
> against it. . . . Revolution in this country of "due process of law"
> would be literally impossible. Whose side would you be on? The
> void of being killed by what is in this country and now knowing
> what is outside of it. (Pp. 39–40)

The context of this assessment, as one might gather from the
essay's title, is America's relationship to the third world. Baraka
insists that no one in the United States has an informed view of
emerging nations. The media, moreover, propagate nothing but
lies about the new people who are coming to power and establish-
ing a more humane way of life. Trapped in this isolationist environment, Baraka felt he had to cultivate an apolitical realm of
higher ideas. When confronted by a radical Mexican delegate to
the Cuban liberation celebration who tells him of America's "irrationality" and blindness, he responds:

> "Look, why jump on me? I understand what you're saying. I'm
> in complete agreement with you. I'm a poet. . . . what can I do?
> I write, that's all. I'm not even interested in politics." (P. 42)

But he soon transcended this void of social and political disinterestedness. He did so through his discovery of the two overriding

aspects of America that keep the country at stalemate. The first was liberalism, and the second was the tokenism this philosophy inspires:

> it is just this group of amateur social theorists, American Liberals, who have done most throughout American history to insure the success of tokenism. Whoever has proposed whatever particular social evasion or dilution — to whatever ignominious end — it is usually the liberal who gives that lie the greatest lip service. They, liberals, are people with extremely heavy consciences and almost nonexistent courage. Too little is always enough. And it is always the *symbol* that appeals to them most. . . . for them "moderation" is a kind of religious catch phrase that they are wont to mumble on street corners even alone late at night. (Pp. 76-77)

The consequences of what he calls the "Liberal/Missionary syndrome" include a falsification of history, a perpetuation of the myth of progress as a way of salving consciences, and the deluding of subjugated peoples through the creation of tokens. These all work against what Baraka considers primary — freedom. White American liberals and their middle-class black advocates, by cleverly subverting the legitimate aspirations of the masses, simply stand in the way of any real movement in society. This is contrary to the natural state of human existence: "A man is either free or he is not. There cannot be any apprenticeship for freedom" (pp. 80-81).

The recommendation that follows Baraka's characterization of the American situation seems inevitable. In "Black Is a Country," he says:

> What I am driving at is the fact that to me the Africans, Asians, and Latin Americans who are news today because of their nationalism, i.e., the militant espousal of the doctrine of serving one's own people's interests before those of a foreign country, e.g., the United States, are exactly the examples the Black man in this country should use in his struggle for independence. (P. 84)

The clear alliance of the black American condition with that of the third-world nations gives these lines a 1950s cast. But Baraka is not simply remarking similarities; he is making a strategic identification. In other words, he is not merely stating that everyone shares a common predicament; he is asserting that black Americans must declare themselves a sovereign state and accept nationalism as a way of achieving complete liberation. His view, of course, runs counter to more moderate positions of the 1950s:

> the struggle moves to make certain that no man has the right to dictate the life of another man. The struggle is not simply for "equality," or "better jobs," or "better schools," and the rest of those half-hearted liberal clichés; it is to completely free the black man from the domination of the white man. Nothing else. . . .
> The Negro's struggle in America is only a microcosm of the struggle of the new countries all over the world. (Pp. 84-85)

At the same time, he, like those of the earlier decade, still suggests a mutual destiny for whites and blacks in America:

> America is as much a black country as a white one. The lives and destinies of the white American are bound up inextricably with those of the black American, even though the latter has been forced for hundreds of years to inhabit the lonely country of black. (P. 85)

Baraka's endorsement of a black separatism in white America was not as firm in 1962 as it was to become later. It was sufficient, however, to motivate his delineation of the center ("City of Harlem"), character ("Street Protest"), and cuisine ("Soul Food") of a sui generis terrain. Moreover, it was strong enough to bring forth revised definitions of art and the function of the artist. The premise of "The Myth of a Negro Literature" is that as a result of their desertion of the emotional references of their own culture and imitation of middle-class white models, black American writers have produced nothing but mediocre works. By contrast: "Negro music . . . , because it drew its strengths and beauties out of the depth of the black man's soul and because to a large extent its traditions could be carried on by the lowest classes of Negroes, has been able to survive the constant and willful dilutions of the black middle class" (p. 106). Baraka logically suggests that black American writers in the future would do well to emulate black jazz and blues musicians. What is particularly striking from the author who saw the poem as a "turning away" is the following conception of serious art:

> High art, first of all, must reflect the experiences of the human being, the emotional predicament of man, as he exists, in the

defined world of his being. . . . High art, and by this I mean any
art that would attempt to describe or characterize some portion
of the profound meaningfulness of human life with any finality
of truth, cannot be based on the superficialities of human existence. It must issue from real categories of human activity, *truthful*
accounts of human life, and not fancied accounts of the attain-
ment of cultural privilege by some willingly preposterous apologists
for one social "order" or another. (P. 109)

Baraka concludes that black American literature has never
fulfilled these conditions because its writers have always accepted
a distorted conception of history rendered by American liberals.
He goes on to assert that Western and American history begin
for the black man with the slave trade (p. 111). Only by going to
the "emotional history of the black man in this country," which
differs from that of the dominant group, can the black writer provide works of cultural relevance (p. 112). If he adopts the prevailing white bourgeois framework, he will not find himself reflected,
because white America does not admit that a *unique* black man—
one unaccounted for by its social codes—exists (p. 113). To accept
such a perspective is to write, Baraka says, "after the fact" (p. 112)
—to take up a life devoid of black cultural significance.

The extension of the foregoing is a view of the virtues of segregation. Because the black American has never been able to cross
that no-man's-land between black and white, he has retained a
specificity of cultural reference that gives "logic and beauty" to his
music (p. 114). This fact, if acknowledged by black writers,
promises an important place in the world for black literature:

At this point when the whole of Western society might go up in
flames, the Negro remains an integral part of that society, but continually outside it, a figure like Melville's Bartleby. He is an American, capable of identifying emotionally with the fantastic cultural
ingredients of this society, but he is also, forever, outside that culture, an invisible strength within it, an observer. If there is ever
a Negro literature, it must disengage itself from the weak, heinous
elements of the culture that spawned it, and use its very existence
as evidence of a more profound America. (Pp. 114–15)

Although the quotation moves in Western and American terms,
it clearly foreshadows Baraka's departure from the West. The

disengagement of black literature could hardly occur without a similar withdrawal by the writer. And the vision of a flaming West foreshadows the projection of an American apocalypse.

By 1962, the careful, reflective, insightful prefigurations were all in order. It should have come as no surprise in 1964, then, to see an essay from Baraka's pen entitled "Last Day of the American Empire (Including Some Instructions for Black People)." The essay concludes:

> The hope is that young blacks will remember all of their lives what they are seeing, what they are witness to just by being alive and black in America, and that eventually they will use this knowledge scientifically, and erupt like Mt. Vesuvius to crush in hot lava these willful maniacs who call themselves white Americans. (P. 209)

The artistic form that will capture this coming Armageddon, says Baraka, is the revolutionary theater:

> The Revolutionary Theatre must teach them [white men] their deaths. It must crack their faces open to the mad cries of the poor. It must teach them about silence and the truths lodged there. It must kill any God anyone names except Common Sense. The Revolutionary Theatre should flush the fags and murders out of Lincoln's face. (P. 211)

It must "show the missionaries and wiggly Liberals dying under blasts of concrete. For sound effects, wild screams of joy, from all the peoples of the world" (p. 211). Adopting the perspective of the victim, the revolutionary theater moves toward change. It is a social art, "where real things can be said about a real world" (p. 212). When fired by imagination, it is almost a mystical enterprise:

> Imagination (Image) is all possibility, because from the image, the initial circumscribed energy, any use (idea) is possible. And so begins that image's use in the world. Possibility is what moves us. (P. 213)

The playwright, therefore, not only assaults whatever runs counter to man's freedom but also provides the necessary images for a transformation of the world. The forceful and aggressive manner in which he portrays society's victims will cause them to rush from the theater and cleanse the universe. When there are no more victims, other heroes will appear in the dramas — revolutionary leaders like Denmark Vesey and Crazy Horse. The stage will be set for the emergence of the "new man" (pp. 214-15). Hence the power of the artistic image properly employed is the power to create a new world.

Baraka calls the writings in *Home* "social essays," and their progression from "Cuba Libre" to "The Revolutionary Theatre" does reflect the tendency (discussed earlier) of black people in American society to raise their arms with ever-increasing force and militancy as the 1960s progressed. Mirroring the "social" mood of the decade, Baraka moved from the bohemian mask of *Preface* to the guise of a writer bringing down the roof beams of an unjust world. His early concern with Western values and literature declined as he adopted a stance more in harmony with the emotional references of his culture — that of rebellious writer. African blues still might not have recognized him, but neither did the radical chic denizens of Bohemia or the casual liberals of the academy. Two 1964 plays — *Dutchman* and *The Slave*[5] — serve to explain this.

Clay — the black protagonist of *Dutchman* — delivers a long, bitter tirade after he and Lula, an archetypal white American woman, have engaged in a series of clever word games. Like the American liberals whom Baraka damns so unequivocally, Lula is a "wiggly" liar caught in her own fantasies of the world. She is also a bohemian figure like the one described in "American Sexual Reference: Black Male": "for the white woman it [being a liberated artist or entertainer] means at one point, that she has more liberal opinions, or at least likes to bask in the gorgeousness of being hip, ok, sophisticated, outcast. There is a whole social grouping of white women who are body-missionaries" (*Home*, p. 223). Unable to avoid myths fostered by the "Liberal/Missionary syndrome" and by the bohemian liberated zone, Clay and Lula have no choice but to pursue their deadly verbal exchange. But the woman pushes too far — to that place where Clay, who has been shedding the bonds of his Western clothing throughout the play, must retaliate in vicious terms. In essence, he tells Lula that all blacks hate all whites, that the proof of this is found in black art, and that once blacks cease to sublimate their anger, they will rise up and murder their white oppressors. The three-piece-suit-wearing black intellectual, who was once so fond of Baudelaire and other white ideas, becomes a poet screaming his madness into the face of the white world. His speech is one act in the revolutionary theater. And his role as a "victim" is dramatically highlighted when he moves to retrieve his belongings from the seat where Lula sits. She stabs him to death.

Though Clay is usually seen as the hero of *Dutchman,* the play's real subject is Lula. Certainly her final action drives home the accuracy of Baraka's 1962 claim that "If, right this minute, I were, in some strange fit of irrationality, to declare that 'I am a free man and have the right of complete self-determination,' chances are that I would be dead or in jail by nightfall" (*Home,* p. 79). The "irrational" black man who asserts his liberation and projects the destruction of America has no place in Lula's scheme of existence except the cemetery or the prison. Yet he is real, and Baraka goes on to picture him in clearer outline in *The Slave.*

Walker Vessels is the black idealist caught in the throes of reconciling his subjective projection of a world more attractive with the bloody mayhem required to translate this vision into actuality. The only thing of which he seems certain is that the white liberal is the major obstacle to the achievement of his goal. In other words, Walker is not as convinced of the undeniable rightness of his own ideas as he is of the undeniable wrongness of his enemy's. One of his exchanges with his white former college professor, Bradford Easley, clarifies this:

> *Easley:* You're so wrong about everything. . . . Do you think Negroes are better people than whites . . . that they can govern a society *better* than whites? . . . So the have-not peoples become the haves. Even so, will that change the essential functions of the world? Will there be more love or beauty in the world . . . more knowledge . . . because of this?
>
> *Walker:* Probably. Probably there will be more . . . if more people have a chance to understand what it is. But that's not even the point. It comes down to baser human endeavor than any social-political thinking. What does it matter if there's more love or

beauty? . . . The point is that you had your chance, darling, now these other folks have theirs. (P. 73)

Easley says in response: "God, what an ugly idea." But Walker insists that it is exactly Easley's kind of brusque and defensive insularity that constitutes the world's ugliness. For Easley is, finally, a man who feels that evil should not be confronted at all but left to die of its own accord. No, says Walker, "right is in the act! And the act itself has some place in the world . . . it makes some place for itself" (p. 75).

Walker contrasts actions with a narrow art when he recalls one of Easley's friends who "hated people who wanted to change the world" (p. 75).

> *Walker:* Yeah, well, I know I thought then that none of you would write any poetry either. I knew that you had moved too far away from the actual meanings of life . . . into some lifeless cocoon of pretended intellectual and emotional achievement, to really be able to see the world again. What was Rino writing before he got killed. Tired elliptical little descriptions of what he could see out the window. (Pp. 75–76)

The dialogue ends when Walker shoots Easley, and the house comes crashing down under the blasts of the liberation army. The idealistic artist turned revolutionary is a startling figure for Easley. And though Walker's attachment to the old days — seen in his attempt to baffle the professor with quotations from Yeats and his concern for his white former wife (Grace) — show through, *The Slave* ends on the last day of the American liberal/intellectual empire.

While both *Dutchman* and *The Slave* were first staged downtown, the progress of the artist revealed by the plays had impelled Baraka uptown — to Harlem. "I don't love you," a poem from *Target Study,* describes his move in powerful terms:[6]

> Whatever you've given me, whiteface glass
> to look through, to find another there, another
> what motherfucker? another bread tree mad at its
> sacredness, and the law of some dingaling god,
>   cold

as ice cucumbers, for the shouters and the
    wigglers,
and what was the world to the words of slick
    nigger fathers,
too depressed to explain why they could not
    appear to be men.

The bread fool. The don'ts of this white hell.
    The crashed eyes
of dead friends, standin at the bar, eyes
    focused on actual ugliness.

I don't love you. Who is to say what that will
    mean. I don't
love you, expressed the train, moves, and uptown
    days later
we look up and breathe much easier

I don't love you

(P. 55)

The certainty that rings through the poem, however, was pur-
chased at an agonizing price, as the 1964 volume of poetry, *The
Dead Lecturer,* illustrates.[7] The title is appropriate, since so many
of the individual poems are concerned with the poet's loss of feeling and the tortures brought on by his severance from his old life.
He speaks, for example, of "The perversity / of separation, isolation, / after so many years of trying to enter their kingdoms"
(p. 29). And the source of human contact seen in *Preface* — the
fingers — is drawn as follows: "(Inside his books, his fingers. They
/ are withered yellow flowers and were never / beautiful)" (p. 15).
The waters, which are viewed as signs of a tangible world containing the possibility of love in the earlier work, have been
transmuted:

(Love twists
the young man. Having seen it
only once. He expected it
to be, as the orange flower
leather of the poet's books.

He expected
less hurt, a lyric. And not
the slow effortless pain
as a new dripping sun pushes
up out of our river.)
       And
having seen it, refuses
to inhale. "It was a
green mist, seemed
to lift and choke
the town."

(P. 17)

The attractive world of his bohemian days has disappeared: "—
They have passed / and gone / whom you thot your lovers"
(p. 31). Finally, the poet can describe himself only as "inside someone who hates me" (p. 15), or as one who is

deaf, and blind and lost and will not
again sing your quiet verse. I have lost
even the act of poetry, and writhe now for cool
horizonless dawn.

(P. 47)

The political poems in *The Dead Lecturer* explore some of the
reasons for his painful condition.

In "A Contract (for the destruction and rebuilding of Pater-
son)," "A Poem for Neutrals," "A Poem for Democrats," and "The
Politics of Rich Painters," Baraka directs pointed attacks at the
corruption of art and life that has resulted from the domination
of the world by the West. To live the chic bohemian life of a
"neutral" artist in the face of this situation would be a betrayal
of one's humanity. Lines from "Green Lantern's Solo" reflect both
the motives for the poet's move to a separate black way of life
in Harlem and the immediate anguish that accompanied it:

What man unremoved from his meat's source,
can continue
to believe totally in himself? Or on the littered
sidewalks of his personal

history, can continue to believe in his own
   dignity or intelligence
Except the totally ignorant
who are our leaders
   Except the completely devious
   who are our lovers.

                            (Pp. 68–69)

The pressing need to be in touch with the "meat's source" forced
him to step beyond the loves and lovers of the past who were ad-
juncts to a sick world. Yet the uncertainty of his transition stands
out in the concluding lines of *The Dead Lecturer:*

When they say, "Is it Roi
who is dead?" I wonder
who will they mean?

                            (P. 79)

Baraka was part of a group of black artists who established
the Harlem Black Arts Repertory Theatre School, an enterprise
devoted to ideas and ideals most effectively set forth in *Home.*
Street theater, creative writing workshops, poetry readings, lectures, exhibitions, and other events designed to heighten the
expressive consciousness of the black urban community were
included in the organization's activities. Baraka asserted that
"Black Art" had now been officially ushered into the world and
securely housed. But he also knew it had come on the winds of
a spiraling nationalism. His 1965 essays in *Home* treat "The
Legacy of Malcolm X, and the Coming of the Black Nation" as
corollaries to an even further revised definition of the black artist.
Malcolm is described as a man who "made the consideration of
Nationalist ideas significant and powerful in our day" (p. 241). He

wanted to give the Nationalistic Consciousness its political embodi-
ment, and send it out to influence the newly forming third world,
in which this consciousness was to be included. The concept of
Blackness, the concept of National Consciousness, the proposal
of a political (and diplomatic) form for this aggregate of Black
spirit, these are the things given to us by Garvey, through Elijah
Muhammed and finally given motion into still another area of Black
response by Malcolm X. (P. 243)

Three concepts are merged under this general conception of nationalism by Baraka: race, nation, and culture. The last is seen as the most pertinent since it constitutes an agency of consciousness:

> What a culture produces, is, and refers to, is an image—a picture of a process, since it is a form of a process: movement seen. The changing of images, of references, is the Black Man's way back to the racial integrity of the captured African, which is where we must take ourselves, in feeling to be truly the warriors we propose to be. (P. 247)

Having emphasized once again the importance of the cultural image, Baraka lays out the following dictates for the black artist:

> The Black Artist's role in America is to aid the destruction of America as we know it. The Black Artist must draw out of his soul the correct image of the world. He must use this image to bond his brothers and sisters together in common understanding of the nature of the world (and the nature of America) and the nature of the human soul. (P. 252)

Both the idea of culture and the specification of the artist's function are rooted in what might be called a sense of black manifest destiny. Baraka says: "God is man realized. The Black Man must realize himself as Black. And idealize and aspire to that" (p. 248). The ultimate goal is a new black humanism. But if the nation can come about only through a cultural consciousness that flows from the soul of the artist, it seems that Baraka is suggesting a conflation of God and the black artist. In other words, the writer is a man like all other men, but one who is more completely realized as God. He becomes, therefore, the leader in a divinely inspired crusade for black cultural nationalism. The difference between Baraka's formulation and, say, James Baldwin's aesthetics, of course, is that the former is fiercely social. It calls for real change in the actual world.

Baraka's revised aesthetic led him in at least two clear "social" directions, yielding first the agitprop dramas of *Four Black Revolutionary Plays* (1969) and *Jello* (1970).[8] With the exception of *A Black Mass,* these works conform closely to the requirements set forth in "The Revolutionary Theatre." In *Experimental Death Unit #1, Great Goodness of Life,* and *Madheart,* black victims are parodied, castigated, or shown in horrible deaths. Duff and Loco, the white characters of *Experimental Death Unit #1,* are appropriately crushed by the bullets of the Black Liberation Army — not before they have been rendered patently grotesque by their dialogue and actions, however. *A Black Mass* stands out from the company because its tone and language are elevated to match a sophisticated ideational framework. The conflict between Jacoub and his fellow "magicians" in the black arts is one between the restless, empirical inventor and the mystical artists who feel their oneness with all things. Finally, Jacoub creates both time and a hideous white beast who adores it under the following sanction: "Let us be fools. For creation is its own end" (p. 24). *A Black Mass* employs the demonology of the Nation of Islam, but in Baraka's hands its story takes on the character of a lyrical, mythopoeic exchange designed to guide the energies of the new Black Arts Movement. The play is dedicated to "the brothers and sisters of The Black Arts." *Jello,* by comparison, is a broad farce designed to show the traditional house servant (in this case, Rochester of the Jack Benny establishment) transforming himself into a revolutionary.

The other direction pursued by Baraka in the years immediately following the establishment of the Black Arts Repertory Theatre School was what might be termed an art of specific recall. Lines from *The Dead Lecturer* project both the style and substance of the form:

> Nothing is ever finished. Nothing past. Each act of my life, with me now, till death. Themselves, the reasons for it. They are stones, in my mouth and ears. Whole forests on my shoulders. (P. 36)

Or:

> What comes, closest is,
> closest. Moving, there
> is a wreck of spirit,
>   a heap of broken feeling. What
> was only love
> or in those cold rooms,
> opinion. Still, it made
> color. And filled me

as no one will. As, even
I cannot fill
myself.

(P. 54)

In a sense, Baraka—like William Carlos Williams, whose work played such a significant role in his early development—is a regional author molding the details of a peculiar New Jersey landscape into an endless variety of meanings. A number of short stories in *Tales* (1967)[9] and the moving autobiographical narration in *The System of Dante's Hell* (1965)[10] are products of an artist who knew his life had been shaped by things as simple as "a green truck." There seems to be a telling personal significance in Walker Vessels' statement that "The aesthete came long after all things that really formed me" (*The Slave,* p. 75).

Baraka uses the cryptic language of the aesthete, however, to sketch those exacting pictures of his school experiences in Newark ("Uncle Tom's Cabin: Alternative Ending," "The Largest Ocean in the World") and his time in the United States Air Force ("Salute") that appear in *Tales.* In these stories, the painful events of his past are rehearsed and mulled over until they yield their precise character. If one sought a definition of this process, it might be Ralph Ellison's definition of the blues, which appears in *Shadow and Act:*

> The blues is an impulse to keep the painful details and episodes of a brutal experience alive in one's aching consciousness, to finger its jagged grain, and to transcend it, not by the consolation of philosophy but by squeezing from it a near-tragic, near-comic lyricism. As a form, the blues is an autobiographical chronicle of personal catastrophe expressed lyrically.[11]

The ending of "Salute," in which the author details his coming into literature and the fanciful world into which he was plunged as a result, seems an apt example. Jolted from his reverie by a lieutenant who says: "Don't you know you're supposed to salute officers?" Baraka describes his response as follows:

> When the focus returned (Mine) I don't know what that means. Focus, returned . . . that's not precise enough. Uh . . . I meant,

when I could finally say something to this guy . . . I didn't have anything to say. But I knew that in the first place. I said, "Yes sir, I know all about it." No, I didn't say any such shit as that. I said, "Well, if the airplanes blow up, Chinese with huge habits will drop out of the sky, riding motorized niggers." You know I didn't say that. But I said something, you know, the kind of shit you'd say, you know. (P. 87)

This is one of the clearer illustrations of Baraka's technique. At times, his references are so intensely personal that it is almost impossible for the reader to grasp them. At such moments, the narrator is the lonely musician riffing to himself. There are a number of instances in *The System of Dante's Hell* where this occurs. But on the whole, the novel offers a stirring and coherent account of the black man who was born into the world "pointed in the right direction." Slowly, though, he moved away from the nurturing sights and smells of his birthplace and into a sterile realm of middle-class pretense and denial. The road he traveled is described by *System* as one that led outward from the childhood gang (The Secret Seven) to places of music and "hip" bell-bottom suits like those portrayed in the chapter entitled "The Christians." College and the air force pushed him even closer to that final, heretical denial that comprises the last chapter of the work:

Fire burns around the tombs. Closed from the earth. A despair came down. Alien grace. Lost to myself, I'd come back. To that ugliness sat inside me waiting. And the mere sky greying could do it. (P. 149)

Having almost surrendered himself to the black South represented by Shreveport's "Bottom," the narrator draws back. He turns inward, and after the fight with three inhabitants of the bottom, in which he is leveled, he somehow manages to get back to his air force base. He awakens three days later with the feeling that his entire experience among the blacks transpired in a cave where he sat reading. The room of *Preface* and Plato's cave of shadows seem to merge here as a sign of the solipsistic artist. But there is a certain tension in the concluding lines of the narrative since the author also seems aware of his role as a blues artist: "I sat reading from a book aloud and they [black people] danced to my

reading" (p. 152). The redemptive value of Baraka's regional and
of his personal art is, perhaps, captured in this image. Stated in
more lyrical terms, it is described by lines from "Leadbelly Gives
an Autograph":

> The possibilities of music. First
> that it does exist. And that we do,
> in that scripture of rhythms. The earth,
> I mean the soil, as melody. The fit you need,
> the throes. To pick it up and cut
> away what does not singularly express.
>
> (*Sabotage,* p. 25)

The poems of *Black Art,* which were written in 1965 and 1966,
the essays of *Raise, Race, Rays, Raze* (1971),[12] and the verse of
Spirit Reach (1972)[13] extend Baraka's previously articulated positions and harmonize disparate tendencies in his work of the mid-
decade. The preoccupation with an art of specific recall, for
example, and revolutionary nationalism combine in Baraka's projection of Newark as the black urban community that will serve
as a model for a new world of black humanism. In "Newark—
Before Black Men Conquered," he begins by analyzing his place
of birth as an example of domestic colonialism:

> There is a clearer feeling in Newark, than any other city I have
> ever been in, of Colonialism. Newark is a *colony.* A bankrupt ugly
> colony, in the classic term, where white people make their money
> to take away with them. (*Raise, Race,* p. 65)

Blacks who inhabit Newark, therefore, are (perforce) separate.
They are not susceptible to American definitions (pp. 78–79). Having continually served as chattel to free men, they must now arise
and seize power over their own domain:

> These cities: Newark, Gary, Washington, Detroit, Richmond,
> Harlem, Oakland, East St. Louis, Bedford-Stuyvesant, etc. any
> large concentration of Black people . . . almost always disunified,
> but these are our kingdoms, and this is where we must first rule.
> . . . The cities must be Black ruled or they will not be ruled at all.
> (P. 79)

The extension of earlier definitions occurs in terms of the spirituality—the manifest destiny—of black America. In "A School
Prayer," a poem from *Black Art,* the poet says:

> The eye sees. The I. The self. Which passes
>   out and into
> the wind. We are so beautiful we talk at the
>   same time
> and our breathing is harnessed to divinity.
>
> (P. 121)

In "The Spell," he continues:

> The eyes of God-our on us
> in us. The Spell, We are wisdom, reaching
>   for itself.
>   We are
> totals, watch us, watch through yourself, and
>   become
>   the whole
> universe at once so beautiful you will become,
>   without having
> moved, or gone through a "change," Except to
>   be moving with the world.
> at that incredible speed, with all the genius
>   of a tree.
>
> (P. 147)

The same theme appears in "The Calling Together":

> Energies exploding
> Black World Renewed
> Sparks! Stars! Eyes!
> Huge Holocausts of Heaven
> Burning down the white man's world
> Holy ashes!!!
> Let the rains melt them into rivers.
> And the new people naked bathe themselves.
> And look upon the life to come as the heaven
>   we
>   seek.
>
> (P. 174)

"Black People: This is our destiny," with its insistence that the rhythms of the "holy black man" are in tune with those of the universe, offers a final example:

> . . . vibration holy nuance beating against
> itself, a rhythm a playing reunderstood now by
>   one of the 1st race
> the primitives the first men who evolve again
>   to civilize
>   the
> world.

(P. 199)

The consciousness needed to effect this destiny, of course, comes from within:

> We are no thing, we are every space
> of living. We are flying without airplanes, cooking
> without stoves. Touch God and know him, look into
> your screaming brain. In those chambers the real
>   way lurks
> in the shadow of your meaningless desires. The
> real breadth of where we move toward, the
>   perfection
> of space.

(P. 209)

Finally, the black poet as the man through whom the divine sanction for a new order flows is seen in lines from "All in the Street":

> Listen to the creator
> speak in me now. Listen, these words
> are part of God's thing. I am a
> vessel, a black priest interpreting
> the present & future for my people
> Olorun—Alah speaks in and
> thru me now . . . He begs me to
> pray for you—as I am doing—He
> bids me have you submit to
> the energy.

(*Spirit Reach,* p. 11)

By the beginning of the 1970s, Baraka could say:

There is no such thing as art and politics, there is only life, and
its many registrations. If the artist is the raised consciousness then
all he touches, all that impinges on his consciousness must be raised.
We must be the will of the race toward evolution. . . . THE LARGEST
WORK OF ART IS THE WORLD ITSELF. The potential is unlimited.
(*Raise, Race,* p. 129)

His voice had become political, saying: "WE MUST BE IN THE REAL
WORLD. WE MUST BE ACTUAL DOERS" (p. 101). In March of 1972,
he was a forceful spokesman at the National Black Political Convention that met in Gary, Indiana, to discuss pragmatic ways to
improve the condition of black people in America. Since that time,
he has moved away from his nationalist stance to endorse what
he calls "Marxism-Leninism-Mao-Tse Tung Thought." Though
Marxism and nationalism are somewhat incompatible, scientific
socialism is a feasible outgrowth of Baraka's spiritual ideals for
the "raised" cultural consciousness and his increasing political involvement in the "real world." In *Raise, Race, Rays, Raze,* he
says: "Do not talk of Marx or Lenin or Trotsky when you speak
of political thinkers" (p. 95). But a reading of his canon reveals
sufficient concern with the economics of colonialism and the politics of national liberation in the third world to provide an explanation of his shift to a Marxist frame of reference. His contact
with Amilcar Cabral and other African socialist thinkers surely
heightened his conviction that the "mystical or cult nationalism
which is not about political struggle" is less effective in the world
at large than a theoretical analysis that begins with the material
base of society.[14] Moreover, a theological stance and a heightened
consciousness have not been at all alien to the actual leaders of
Marxism-Leninism or Maoist thought in our day. One of the most
significant aspects of Baraka's change of loyalties, of course, is
that it reflects the growing disenchantment with a strict cultural
nationalism that has characterized black America since 1973. His
is but one of the many revised or altered strategies adopted by
blacks in the lean, quiet years since Watergate. Nonetheless, one
has the feeling that his current position augurs war no less surely
than his position of a few years back:

we [advocates for a new communist party] represent working people
and oppressed nationalities who when they find out what has to
be done, that a revolution is what is needed, will sweep all slow
babblers and jivers aside and destroy all forms of oppression and
exploitation by means of the armed seizure of state power.[15]

The man who was "thinking of a dance" at the beginning of the
1960s has found the music:

BANZAI!!   BANZAI!!   BANZAI!!   BANZAI!!
came running out of the drugstore with
an electric alarm clock, and then dropped the
    motherfucker
and broke it. Go get something else. Take
    everything
    in there.
Look in the cashregister. TAKE THE MONEY. TAKE
    THE MONEY.
    YEH.
TAKE IT ALL. YOU DONT HAVE TO CLOSE THE DRAWER.
    COME ON MAN, I SAW
A TAPE RECORDER BACK THERE.
These are the words of lovers
Of dancers, of dynamite singers
These are songs if you have the
music.

                                    (*The Slave,* p. 104)

V

Critical Change and Blues Continuity: An Essay on the Criticism of Larry Neal

When he became commissioner of arts for the District of Columbia, Larry Neal, the coeditor of *Black Fire,* was no longer a Black Aesthetician. In fact, he had written more than one essay suggesting that the legacy of that aesthetic — its defensive chauvinism and mystical reliance on "race" — was detrimental to the progress of both black literature and criticism. Neal's new position was troubling to me because it objectified my own. As a well-salaried academic in an Ivy League university, I could scarcely claim that I was the same militant denouncer of all things white who had chanted loudly outside a Charlottesville jail about the unjust incarceration of black "political prisoners."

In the ranks of the Black Aesthetic, what occurred during the mid-seventies was a slip behind the back of consciousness like those discussed by Hegel in the *Phenomenology.* Such slips are unobserved transformations of self in the dialectics of the spirit.

The charge of apostasy leveled at any former member of the Black Aesthetic has, often, been merely a stunned response to his objectification of one's other self emergent from the blind side of one's own spirit. The apostate — lo-and-behold — is simply one's "self-already-moved."

Neal was objectively and coolly representative of transformations that led Baraka to Marxism, Sonia Sanchez to the Nation of Islam, and me to the realms of literary theory. Having commenced as avowed guerrilla theater revolutionaries, we found ourselves, suddenly, playing to respectable houses whose paying audiences eagerly awaited our next scenes. These audiences, by any objective count, were predominantly white. That is to say, only a serious fantasy could sustain the notion that the intended readers of a book like my theoretical work *The Journey Back* (1980) were members of the black masses.

No, on what Baraka calls "the real side," many of us would have been forced to admit that our Black Aesthetic efforts had won the most gratifying applause possible: emulation by a minority audience *and* acceptance by an extensive and enthusiastic white audience.

Neal left the Black Aesthetic, at least in part, because he began to read extensively and enthusiastically in literary criticism and theory. Like many of us, he began to search for viable models of black criticism and theory. Readers who were not white and male, circa 1964–65, had begun to feel that the standard story of "American" literature told by traditional criticism was weak and weary, tired and dreary. There were also a number of nontraditional white critics who found the extant critical hegemonies bothersome. Fredric Jameson, Hillis Miller, Ralph Cohen, Geoffrey Hartman come immediately to mind. They all acknowledged French, German, Eastern European (the legacy of the Russian Formalists and the Prague Linguistic Circle), and Swiss (the Geneva School) critical and theoretical models. They called for a rewriting of familiar notions of genre and canons. They also recuperated work of critics such as Walter Benjamin and Christopher Caudwell. It was an exciting time.

It was also a time that demanded from white and black critics alike better definitions of the nature of expressive cultural traditions. No longer would a mystically black "beauty" or an equally mysterious "manifest" white American destiny suffice to explain the peculiarity of literary works of art. The times — at least in part as a redaction of a revolutionary fervor marking American life in general — demanded new explanatory models that would rewrite literary history as *New Literary History, Glyphs, Diacritics, Poetics Today,* or, at least, *Critical Inquiry.*

I like now to think that Neal wanted to offer a more "scientific" approach to Afro-American literary study — not unlike the "scientific socialism" of Baraka or the more empirical black literary "theory" being called for by an emergent group of Afro-American critics at Yale. To "shake it up baby" in the world of expressive cultural study in the mid-seventies was not simply to proclaim "black is beautiful." The job was, in the words of one of the black Yale critics, to learn how "to pass from metaphor to metaphor and from image to image of the same metaphor in order to locate the Afro-American *genius loci,*" and to learn "to move freely throughout the full compass of the Afro-American *temenos,* from the *genius loci* at the center to the outermost reaches of the *temenos* circumference." This, indeed, was a new order of critical language and enterprise! It was the order of the day when Neal became commissioner of arts. His visiting professorship at Yale must surely have influenced more than one decision and definition in the commissioner's office.

Having posed questions in the early seventies about how, precisely, to substantiate claims for a distinctive Afro-American culture and literature as American realities, I organized during my first year as director of Afro-American Studies at the University of Pennsylvania (1974–75) a symposium entitled "The Function of Black Criticism at the Present Time." I assembled African, Caribbean, and Afro-American writers and scholars. Our aim was to formulate an adequate, accurate, and empowering explanatory model for the study of black literature. The proceedings of our symposium were published as *Reading Black: Essays in the Criticism of African, Caribbean, and Black American Literature* (1976). Though the volume, which commences with an essay by Nobel laureate Wole Soyinka, is proclaimed as an extension of the Black Aesthetic, it is, in fact, evidence of my self-already-moved — toward theory.

And it was, finally, in the movement toward theory that I encountered Larry Neal once again after my first discovery of him as a Black Aesthetician. It was not in Neal's rewrite of a houndstooth jacket and buckled shoes that mark his picture on the dust jacket of *Black Fire* (Baraka wears a dashiki and a scowl) that

I recognized the former Black Aesthetician. It was not, that is to say, the commissioner's suit and appearance of respectability that struck an accord between what I recognized as my own rewritten self and that of Neal. Rather, what brought recognition was *sound*. I found Neal again by listening to the blues — his, mine, OURS. What he called the "blues God" had become my own privileged inscription of "renaissancism" by the time I wrote the following essay.

Rather than *apostasy,* I now believe that Larry's move was to become commissioner of the blues. And by 1983, I had myself begun to hear blues as a changing-same matrix for moving us on from stultifying fixity and chauvinistic repetitions of black beauties. The blues seemed to me the prod and spur that compelled us to "get away" from any position — literary critical or culturally political — that failed to raise oppressive heels from our collective neck.

I know that what I, like the poor pilgrim traveler of the sorrow songs, found in my movement away from the Black Aesthetic was that the voyage out is, always already, the journey back. It is an eternal return to the source, where one not only *meets* but also, in sometimes startling ways, *hears* one's own soul singing.

Larry was ourselves — singing SOS — the same old spirited stuff that has allowed us not only to come out from under the yoke but also to take a lead position (VOICE) that even whites, on the two-way boulevards of American culture, have followed.

Commissioner of the arts. Singer of the blues. Who possibly could have projected such a signal conflation and outcome of the Black Aesthetic? And who might more gratefully write about it than a theorist of the blues?

since life is change . . . art must be change. There is no need to worry
about permanence in the sense that things can be deep frozen forever. The universe is in motion. If this is the case, what is the function of criticism? It is merely a way into things. And it is important
only insofar as it relates to the nature of the changing world. There
are, consequently, no steadfast critical values.

—Larry Neal

 Even in the stormy days of the late 1960s, when injunctions to guard the revolutionary parapets were as
persistent as the sound tracks are in the Atlanta air-
port's sterile transportation mall, there always seemed to be time
for freedom fighters or cultural liberators to step inside for a
moment to enlighten the intellectually curious. The common room
of a residential college at Yale was the scene for one such moment,
and the black artist in performance was Larry Neal. Eyes squinted,
body attuned to the voice of his blues god, he held the audience
(most of them black) in thrall. Deceptively youthful in appearance, he filled the room with old rhythms and venerable lore. He
became a transformed being, a priest intoning black mysteries.
A poem that I wrote on the occasion of his untimely death in 1981
captures my sense of his Yale performance.[1] The opening lines
read as follows:

I remember your strut.
Disguised as Garvey's ghost,
You entered the room.
Your plumed stride and narrow eyes
Matched the peacock's radiant glory.
You gave the shout of Shine,
Bellowed like James Brown,
Swam miraculously against the white currents.

As poet and literary critic, Neal worked from the beginning
years of the sixties to define and further the aims of the Black
Arts and Black Aesthetic projects. What moves preeminently
through his early creative and critical efforts is a nationalistic spirit,
a sense that a unique, separatist ethos is eternally at work among
Afro-America's masses. Marcus Garvey and the Universal Negro
Improvement Association were his early-twentieth-century

exemplars of a black nationalist ethos, although he acknowledged nineteenth-century spokespersons such as Edward Blyden and Martin Delany as Garvey's forebears. A nationalist separatism in politics and social organization, however, was for Neal only a beginning. Without *nationalism in culture,* he believed, there existed no possibility for social change. A meaningful program for social change would have to weld politics and culture, social organization and expressive awareness. In his opinion, Garvey's ideal of self-determination for the masses was hopelessly hamstrung by the West Indian leader's reverence for European expressive form.[2] Conversely, the cultural nationalism implicit in Alain Locke's aesthetically revolutionary document *The New Negro* (1925) was sharply bracketed by that work's failure to recognize or speak to specific social, political, and economic needs of the black masses.[3] Hence, the Black Arts and Black Aesthetic projects of the 1960s and 1970s sought to move with a hip, politically effective stride akin to Garvey's—full of plumed glory and proud display. (Check out the bannered opening day exercises led by LeRoi Jones and Hampton Clanton down 125th Street when the Black Arts Repertory Theatre School was christened in 1965.) Both projects also sought, however, to take full account of vibrant Afro-American cultural forms—the latest manifestations of a racial spirit and memory—propelling the masses in their Shine(ing) swim against main currents in American thought.

To shout like James ("Say it loud!") Brown, and in that shouting attain respectful attention from a black audience aware that you (the shouter) had mastered apt cultural compulsives, was the sole revolutionary necessity for Larry Neal. In his own person, he was a captivating shouter, a cool welder of cultural compulsives, a master of the urban hipster's subtle effrontery and surprising knowledge. He could quote Karl Marx and Malcolm X in the same paragraph, detailing between the lines the social-realist norms implied by the former and mythico-ritualistic criteria mandated by the latter. Like his ever-synthesizing style, his intellectual program was flexible. He could absorb diverse postulates, creating a discourse that fairly hummed with tensions. Amiri Baraka has designated him a "wailer," and, indeed, the sobriquet seems just. For he was always like a musician straining for infinite reaches of sound in a finite universe. His tendency was to impro-

Larry Neal

vise strenuously on a limited set of themes, working them tire-
lessly until their implications were manifest to even the very hard
of hearing.

And, yes, I mean to suggest *repetitiousness* as a distinguishing
trait of his oeuvre. He returns time and again to such preoccupa-
tions as *function* versus *craft* in the artistic domain, the necessity
for cultural spokespersons to comprehend the "living culture" of
their group, the relationship between Afro-American and Western
expressive forms and values, the contours and limitations of black
nationalism as a basis for social theory and change. One recur-
ring figure lending cohesiveness to his criticism is the Afro-American novelist Ralph Ellison. His persistent engagement with Ellison
becomes, in a paradoxical way, a trope for *change,* or, one might
say, a metaphor for the necessity of critical change.

Critics of traditional American literature have often spoken
of Herman Melville's quarrel with God (and, more recently, with
fiction) as a leitmotif of that nineteenth-century writer's corpus.
The unity of Neal's criticism consists, at least in part, of his inces-

sant worrying of an Ellisonian line. If there is one clear anxiety in his cultural riffings, it is the unmitigated influence of Ralph Waldo Ellison.

Reviewing Ellison's collection of essays *Shadow and Act* in the year of their publication (1964), Neal wrote:

> There is no escaping it, Ellison is one of the best novelists of our time. . . . In terms of the positive needs of the black writer, there is much to be gained from reading these essays, because they affirm the richness of the Afro-American tradition and give the potential writer hints as to how this tradition organically functions in a work of art.[4]

However, Ellison's orientation toward European culture and his inclination to read simultaneously texts of Western and Afro-American expression (to "share corn bread with Jimmy Rushing and Jascha Heifetz") make him, in Neal's estimates, a too glib "Renaissance" man. The reaches of a sensibility educated in Western lore, suggests Neal, are wide of the mark aspired to by Black Arts writers who strive for a specificity of cultural referents and performance that brings them into affective contact with a mass audience. Hence, such writers shy away from an Ellisonian emphasis on craft. "We refuse to produce work," says Neal, "that sacrifices moral commitment for something called 'craft'" (p. 28). "Function" is the Black Arts alternative to craft:

> The real issue, as I see it, is the function of art, not in the Marxist sense which also proves to be inadequate for us, but in the sense that what is expressed is felt. And, as in jazz, there is a unity between the audience and the performer. This is the relationship many black writers are searching for today. (P. 28)

What is implied by these remarks is a *feeling sense of form* that derives from an understanding of black cultural compulsives combined with moral commitment to the desires of an Afro-American community. The jazz musician as model suggests a kind of expressive liminal heroism that offers affective (as opposed to economic, political, or, even, physical) liberation.

There scarcely seems to be a positive advantage, though, in dropping requirements of "craft" only to achieve a putatively "functional" affective bonding. Cultural hero and cultural audience may come together in bright beams of sound, to be sure, but to what end? Neal's first encounter with the Ellisonian literary lion in his path produced an intriguing suggestion about the black artist's reference public, but it yielded little in the way of specifics on how expressive forms created without due attention to craft might function in a morally committed (or politically effective) manner. Ellison's achievement stands in bold relief, therefore, against the reviewer's wistfully unspecific projections of a blacker and more dedicatedly moral art. Which is merely to note that, like most critics who are also artists, Neal self-consciously chose his own peculiar set of artistic problems in advance of any clear notions about their probable solution. The initial step in arriving at solutions has traditionally been a rounding up of collegial allies. Once allies are chosen, it is easier to identify what the poet Don L. Lee (Haki Madhubuti) calls "the real enemy." "If you are not part of the solution," wrote Celie's predecessor in pants manufacture, "you are part of the problem."

In the June 1965 issue of *Liberator* magazine, Neal proclaimed a black "cultural front" (a *scene,* as it were, for new forms of Afro-American assertiveness) as a Harlem reality.[5] The basis for his proclamation consisted of two events: a weekend conference on the role of the Afro-American artist held at a fraternity house and the opening of the Black Arts Repertory Theatre School. These events, he suggests, since they were staged in Harlem and played to a community audience, signal the community's realization that "cultural aspects" of black life are essential to any effective black political strategy: "One of the most direct avenues of arriving at a political understanding of the Afro-American is through his culture; specifically artistic culture" (p. 26). Black artists, their mass constituency, and black political leaders must unite; they must address themselves to collective black needs and refuse to be constrained by dictates of a "dominant white society which is responsible for . . . [their] alienation in the first place" (p. 27). With will (and strokes of the pen), Neal thus creates a *scene,* a community, an audience, and fellow creative travelers as allies in the Black Arts enterprise.

After allies comes a revisionist reading of established canons. That is to say, one must take on the enemy by claiming that a legitimate line of succession runs through one's own, as opposed to his, vein of reasoning.

In several essays written between 1965 and 1966, Neal analyzes the efforts of Richard Wright, Ralph Ellison, and others in order to demonstrate the historical legitimacy of the Black Arts project. One of the fundamental problems for the black writer in American society, he asserts, has been a "confusion about function rather than a confusion about form."[6] Wright, however, understood how such confusion might be avoided. In his 1937 essay "Blueprint for Negro Writing," he clearly stated that it is always necessary for an Afro-American writer nationalistically to engage living folk forms of the black community if he or she is to be an effective agent of change. In Neal's view, therefore, Wright accepted "his responsibility to his people," seeking to reconcile black nationalism and communism in a strategy designed to produce an art leading to sociopolitical action: "The nationalism that Wright is concerned with is a nationalism of action" (p. 22). By contrast, Ralph Ellison is limited as an artist by "Western critical theories"; he is constrained by "forms imposed from without" and, thus, implicitly endorses a "non-functional, actionless concept of literary art" (p. 20). The (W)right line, therefore, runs through Black Arts reasoning because this project is actional, nationalistic, and community oriented. Ellison's project is inauthentic; he is merely a pretender to the communal throne.

What makes an adversary a valued one, though, is the tension he or she creates. The opposition remains loyal only so long as it maintains an expected tension on the line. In January 1966, one finds Neal again engaged with Ellison on (by now) familiar issues.[7] Having conceded that the author of *Invisible Man* possesses a brilliant grasp of the folk repertoire of black America, Neal adduces additional grounds for his quarrel with his elder. More white than black readers profit from Ellison's fiction because he has not placed his creativity where "his people" can reach it. Though the novelist appropriates Afro-American cultural forms with consummate skill, he fails to return this cultural heritage to "his people" in a manner supportive of their liberation. Ellison, in Neal's view, seems steadfastly to refuse to articulate the implications of black folk forms for theories and strategies of black political liberation. Neal directs the following injunction (and implicit plea) to the older writer:

> The myth and folklore, that you write about Ellison, must be turned inward and explored in all of its dimensions by our own people.

For you are talking to white people about a humanity, the existence
of which, some Negroes question themselves. Hence, your art will
die, unless, you can bring it to us, to our institutions, to our paltry
literary adventures, to our movements, and counter movements.
(P. 11)

Neal does not ask Ellison to relinquish his craft, his folk
sources, or his creative vision. He merely calls upon the older
author to end his apparent isolation from the quotidian political
and psychological needs of an oppressed people. One irony of
his plea, however, is its tacit recognition that Ellison stands apart
because "literary adventures in the black community" are *paltry*.
That is to say, Neal forthrightly acknowledged that Ellisonian production and readership in Afro-America at large are inconceiv-
able. In a 1967 *Negro Digest* essay entitled "The Black Musician
in White America," he wrote: "Most of the Black communities
of America have not developed the cultural institutions that would
sustain and develop a legitimate artistic expression."[8] This claim
suggests a further irony. For in his essay, he is addressing the
failure of black America to sustain modern jazz as "legitimate"
artistic expression. But if jazz is, nevertheless, sustained (as it certainly has been), who has provided its legitimacy? One answer
is: white America. How, then, can jazz constitute legitimate black
"community" expression? There is further irony still. For the expression that Afro-America does endorse seems to be considered
artistically illegitimate by Neal.

That is to say, although James Brown and the Supremes speak
to the desires of the black community, they are considered inadequate for a nation that possesses jazz potential and Ellisonian
rhetorical resourcefulness. Neal seems to rate Ellison and jazz as
higher and more effective forms of Afro-American expression —
despite their putative "illegitimacy." His Western axiological leanings stand in bold relief.

The motives behind his ironies, however, are economic. Like
many thousands gone before, he finds himself confronted by the
necessity of imagining or defining a new communal black art form
that can reconcile exigencies of economic production and support
with Ellisonian genius *and* black popular expressive taste. A formidable task! Like a group of talented playwrights who worked
during the 1960s and 1970s, however, he felt that he had dis-

covered such a form in the revolutionary, black theater. His most
assured essay on behalf of the Black Arts project is entitled "The
Black Arts Movement" and appeared in the *Tulane Drama Review*
during the summer of 1968.[9] The essay contains the following well-
known statement:

> The Black Arts Movement is radically opposed to any concept of
> the artist that alienates him from his community. Black Art is the
> aesthetic and spiritual sister of the Black Power concept. As such,
> it envisions an art that speaks directly to the needs and aspirations
> of Black America. In order to perform this task, the Black Arts
> Movement proposes a radical reordering of the western cultural
> aesthetic. It proposes a separate symbolism, mythology, critique,
> and iconology. The Black Arts and the Black Power concept both
> relate broadly to the Afro-American's desire for self-determination
> and nationhood. Both concepts are nationalistic. One is concerned
> with the relationship between art and politics: the other with the
> art of politics. (P. 272)

This statement is one of the more coherent and idealistic definitions of a black revolutionary aesthetic to emerge from the sixties.
It suggests a merger in which "ethics and aesthetics . . . interact
positively and . . . [are] consistent with the demands for a more
spiritual world" (p. 275). For "A profound ethical sense . . . makes
a Black artist question a society in which art is one thing and the
actions of men another" (p. 275). Hence, art and experience are
inextricably wedded; positive art is, in fact, positive social action.
The theater, therefore, is the acme of a legitimate Black Arts
project:

> For theater is potentially the most social of all the arts. It is an
> integral part of the socializing process. It exists in direct relation-
> ship to the audience it claims to serve. (P. 279)

Represented by dramas of LeRoi Jones, Ron Milner, Jimmy
Garrett, and Ben Caldwell—dramas such as *Dutchman* that were
acclaimed on "scenes" other than Harlem—the black theater constitutes "the basis for a viable movement in the theatre—a movement which takes as its task a profound reevaluation of the black
man's presence in America" (p. 290).

Neal's nationalistic voice thus discovers an artistic object that satisfies his activist criteria. What Jones calls a "theater of victims" — one that moves oppressed people to action against their oppressors — is the epitome of black artistic form. Paradoxically, Jones's plays received their highest accolades in off-Broadway production; their valorization came not from "victims" rushing into the streets with intense fury but from presenters of coveted Obie Awards. Once again, Neal's preferences and those of more traditional, white evaluators coalesce.

I do not want my assessment of Neal's posture in "The Black Arts Movement" to sound uncharitable. The essay speaks eloquently for itself. I do wish to indicate, however, that he progressively distances himself from the clenched militancy of the early sixties as he confronts the very real exigencies of making black art viable in America. From a fine contempt for craft and a sharp skepticism before the works of Ralph Ellison, he moves to the stirring formulations of "The Black Arts Movement," only to find himself recommending dramas that have been lauded for their craft and for what one might call their "Ellisonian comprehensiveness."

After "The Black Arts Movement," Neal effectively abandons his quarrel with Ellison. The former enemy becomes, in fact, the hero of his 1970 essay "Ellison's Zoot Suit."[10] Published in *Black World,* the opening lines of the essay acknowledge that most criticism directed at the author of *Shadow and Act* "emanates from ideological sources that most of us today reject" (p. 58). "Social realist" premises, according to Neal, have led to inadequate evaluations of Ralph Ellison who (unlike Richard Wright) understands symbolic, mythic, and ritualistic depths that lie behind a zoot suit's fastidiously stylish surface. Ellison, in designing his own unique zoot suit of creativity, "developed a new aesthetic universe, one that was seeking to develop its own laws of form and content . . . [a universe characterized by] the free play of fantasy and myth" (p. 62). Finally, according to Neal: "Ellison's vision, in some respects, is not that far removed from the ideas of some of the best black writers and intellectuals working today" (p. 63). Hence the former outsider, the man removed from the community and threatened with the certain demise of his work, is gathered into the fold as a black cultural nationalist, a "counter-Marxian" striving assiduously against social-realist norms, a harbinger of a theory of culture able to lend clarity to the quest for Afro-American liberation. Ellison's keen awareness that "the Lindy-hop and the zoot suit are . . . not merely social artifacts . . . but . . . , in fact, mask deeper levels of symbolic and social energy" (p. 68) is the type of cognizance required to produce a new and effective leadership for the black community. And Ellison's craft is adduced as one key to his cultural awareness. By mastering the instruments of European culture he managed to produce a sui generis aesthetic outcome. "That trumpet you got in your hand may have been made in Germany," writes Neal, "but you sure sound like my Uncle Rufus whooping his coming-home call across the cotton fields" (p. 76). Finally, Ellison is seen as an artist who has "taken the other dude's instruments" and used them to play his own spiritually rooted black song. He exemplifies the artist as synthesizer, working with the "accumulated weight of . . . Western experience" to produce an effectively ritualistic and political art (pp. 78–79).

If it sounds as though Neal executes a radical *volte-face* in "Ellison's Zoot Suit," then I have succeeded in my analysis. I believe that he was undone by the obvious pitfalls and clear financial failings of so many enterprises conceived by the Black Arts and Black Aesthetic projects. By 1970, he deemed it necessary to project a different vision. He chose an obviously successful model in Ralph Ellison and substituted embracement for anxiety in the face of his influential predecessor. His work of the 1970s moves away from the "parochialism" of a militant separatism to championship of a "new nationalism" devoted to challenging "the establishment theater."[11] Instead of withdrawing from Western art, black artists must confront it. "Remember how black sound dominates the American musical sensibility," he enjoins in his 1972 essay "Into Nationalism, Out Of Parochialism."[12] "Part of what we should do now is take on the American theater sensibility and replace it with ours. Or, at least, place our statement in the arena" (p. 102). What is implied in the essay is a pluralism of cultural imperatives operative in the very definition of America and in the broad arena of American art. Clearly this is a type of critical vision that no one has been more eloquent in articulating than Ralph Ellison.

Neal's new view for the seventies suggests that an artist or a critic must combine sensitivity to his cultural heritage with a sharp knowledge of the general artistic limits and possibilities surrounding such a heritage. One must compete in world-class competition to register—indeed, to impress—one's own unique vision on the cosmos. Certainly a defensive nationalism (one predicated on a feared destruction of one's culture by the mainstream) cannot achieve the critical or creative postures requisite for a new vision. One of Neal's most thoughtful and scholarly essays is designed, I think, as a corrective for a limiting aesthetic perspective in the study of art and culture in America.

Entitled "The Black Contribution to American Letters: Part II, The Writer as Activist—1960 and After," the essay appeared (as a complement to Langston Hughes's "Part I") in *The Black American Reference Book,* edited by Mabel Smythe and published in 1976.[13] In the essay, Neal identifies the Black Aesthetic's interest in an African past and in African-American folklore as a species of Herderian nationalism and goes on to say:

> Nationalism, wherever it occurs in the modern world, must legitimize itself by evoking the muse of history. This is an especially necessary step where the nation or group feels that its social oppression is inextricably bound up with the destruction of its traditional culture and with the suppression of that culture's achievements in the intellectual sphere.

A social group's reaction in such nationalistic instances, according to Neal, is understandably (though also regrettably) one of total introspection—i.e., it withdraws into itself and labels the historically oppressive culture as "the enemy" (p. 782). A fear of the destruction of Afro-American culture by an "aggressive and alien" West, for example, prompted Black Aesthetic spokespersons to think only in racial terms and to speak only in "strident" tones as a means of defending their culture against what they perceived as threats from the West. Such a strategy, however, in Neal's view, represents a confusion of politics and art, an undesirable conflation of the "public" domain of social activism and the "private" field of language reserved for artistic creation and literary-theoretical investigation.

Such a response is, in his estimation, finally a form of distorted

"Marxist literary theory in which the concept of race is substituted for the Marxist idea of class" (p. 783). The attempt to apply
the "Ideology of race to artistic creation" (p. 784), he says, is
simply a contemporary manifestation of Afro-American literature's (and, by implication, Afro-American literary criticism's) historical dilemma:

> The historical problem of black literature is that it has in a sense
> been perpetually hamstrung by its need to address itself to the ques-
> tion of racism in America. Unlike black music, it has rarely been
> allowed to exist on its own terms, but rather [has] been utilized
> as a means of public relations in the struggle for human rights.
> Literature can indeed make excellent propaganda, but through
> propaganda alone the black writer can never perform the highest
> function of his art: that of revealing to man his most enduring
> human possibilities and limitations. (P. 784)

In order to perform the "highest function" of artistic creation
and criticism the black spokesperson must concentrate his attention and efforts on "method" — on "form, structure, and genre" —
rather than on "experience" or "content" (pp. 783–84). Neal, therefore, who called in the sixties for a literature and criticism that
spoke "directly to the needs and aspirations of Black America," ends
his later essay by calling for a creativity that projects "the accumulated weight of the world's aesthetic, intellectual, and historical
experience" as a function of its mastery of "form." His revised,
formalist position leads not only to a condemnation of the critical
weaknesses of former allies in the Black Aesthetic camp but also
to a valorization of the theoretical formulations of such celebrated
"Western" theoreticians as Northrop Frye and Kenneth Burke
(pp. 783–84). Neal never criticized Ralph Ellison for a lack of
Afro-American cultural knowledge. He never felt that Ellison was
uninformed; he simply believed that the author of *Invisible Man*
had been misdirected by dictates of Western literary critics and
cultural theorists. But in the final analysis, Neal himself opens
his arms to embrace not only Ellison but also the impressive
parade of literary-critical "others" who follow in his wake.

In "Cultural Nationalism and Black Theatre," a 1968 essay,
Neal writes:

since life is change . . . art must be change. There is no need to worry about permanence in the sense that things can be deep frozen forever. The universe is in motion. If this is the case, what is the function of criticism? It is merely a way into things. And it is important only insofar as it relates to the nature of the changing world. There are, consequently, no steadfast critical values.[14]

(Barbara Herrnstein Smith could not have said it better, or sooner.) Neal moved with the changes of a universe of artistic, cultural, and literary-theoretical discourse characterizing his epoch. And he clearly stood closer to a camp of sophisticated polemics by the time of his *Black American Reference Book* essay.

Yet it seems important to query whether the principle (what an older descriptive mode would have called "the virtue") of Neal's criticism can be confined to "change." Does his importance as a critic reside exclusively in the example he provided of a querulous nationalist giving way before rigors of expressive production and survival in America to a more sophisticated Western view of the arts? (And it is remarkable how many theoretical moves of the current generation of Afro-Americanists in the United States were anticipated by Neal.) Is it of paramount importance, finally, that Neal focused a major share of his critical attention on Ralph Ellison, who stands as metaphor for his own evolving critical consciousness?

Any importance that we ascribe to "change" in Neal's critical oeuvre (or to his quarrel with Ellison) must be coextensive with the significance we grant to *continuity* in his corpus. That continuity is a function of Neal's unequivocal certainty that his evaluation of Afro-American blues was timely and indisputably accurate.

The line that Neal endorsed as a critic finds its origin not in the United States of the sixties (though this site is surely his own most frequently privileged locus) but rather in an Africa of the critical imagination. He takes Ellison to task because the Ellisonian line is so firmly anchored among what the sage John Ruskin called "the stones of Venice." A measure of the tension between Neal and his influential predecessor results from the different genealogies their divergent lines assign to the blues. For Ellison, the blues are a secular, expressive, autobiographical manifestation of black culture in America. While their analogue is not European philosophy, it is

European folk music—specifically, Spanish flamenco. For Neal, the blues are extensions of an African spiritual pantheon in the New World. Their analogues are entirely black, and sacred. The line of descent suggested by Neal is captured in his 1972 essay "Any Day Now: Black Art and Black Liberation":

> The Black Church . . . represents and embodies the transplanted African memory. The Black Church is the Keeper . . . [of the memory of the Motherland], the spiritual bank of our most forgotten visions of the Homeland. The Black Church was the institutionalized form that Black people used to protect themselves from the spiritual and psychological brutality of the slavemaster . . . , [and] at the pulsating core of their emotional center, the blues are the spiritual and psychological brutality of the slavemaster . . . , of life's raw realities. Even though they appear primarily to concern themselves with the secular experience, the relationships between males and females, between boss and worker, between nature and Man, they are, in fact, extensions of the deepest, most pragmatic spiritual and moral realities. Even though they primarily deal with the world as flesh, they are essentially religious. Because they finally celebrate life and the ability of man to control and shape his destiny.[15]

In "Some Reflections on the Black Aesthetic" (1970), Neal situates the black church's origins in "Spirit worship, orishas, ancestors, African Gods."[16] And the transmitters of African sacred energies are defined as priests, houngans, and preachers whose lineage continues through conjurers, soothsayers, and seers to blues men and women as poets, rappers, and moral judges in a rocking world of popular entertainment. Blues—always the blues and its singers—stand as modal norms for the public person of Afro-American culture—whether that figure is a preacher, politician, or poet. For the blues' awesome genealogy makes them the signally legitimate expressive form of Afro-American culture. They are God-given, God-bearing resonances that survived the Middle Passage and provided coherence for black experience in the New World. In a 1978 interview with Lisa DiRocco, Neal said:

> So, that's *my* metaphor—the blues god—it's not nobody else's metaphor. It's mine. . . . The blues god is an attempt to isolate the blues element as an ancestral force, as the major ancestral force

of the Afro-American. What I always say about the blues god is that it was the god that survived the middle passage. It's like an *Orisha* figure. Because even though the blues may be about so-called hard times, people generally feel better after hearing them or seeing them. They tend to be ritually liberating in that sense.[17]

Blues, then, offer ancestrally legitimate instances of an African spirit at work; they are everywhere infused with the quotidian rituals of Afro-American life on New World shores. They are, in fact, an epic cycle of everyday life organically related through their various performers and practitioners to black culture:

> Taken together . . . the blues represent an epic cycle of awesome proportions — one song (poem) after the other expressing the daily confrontations of Black people with themselves and the world. They are not merely entertainment. They act to clarify and make more bearable the human experience, especially when the context of that experience is oppressive. A man that doesn't watch his "happy home" is in a world of trouble.[18]

Hence the blues singer is "not an alienated artist moaning songs of self-pity and defeat to an infidel mob. He is the voice of the community, its historian, and one of the shapers of its morality."[19]

In sharp contrast to Neal's reverential view of the blues as a consummate expressive spiritual form to be emulated, Ellison's definition takes blues as a secular starting point, an interesting pad from which to launch missilic flights into High Art. What separates Ellison and Neal most decisively as black spokespersons is Neal's blues continuities. He was compelled by the evolving/changing critical discourse of his era to go through changes, but in the synapses of all those connections made with Western thought were sounds of an African/Caribbean/New World/Afro-American/Funky-But/Downhome/Journeyed-Back/Gut-Bucket/Honky Tonk *changing same* called the blues. Stabilizing all New World changes in Neal's view — as in the view of thousands gone before him — were the blues. He was a person who recommended James Brown and Aretha Franklin, Barbecue Bob and Bo Diddley, Otis Redding and Shine, Sugar Ray and the Signifying Monkey for our consideration as *blues norms* in the creation and judgment of a legitimate Afro-American expressivity. As such, he was a pivotal figure in the evolution of a vernacular, blues theory of Afro-American expression in the United States. He worried an Ellisonian line so persistently because he knew that Ellison was a mighty instrument of the blues god confused about where all the good love and feelin' that he poured into *Invisible Man* came from. ("Calling Ralph Ellison. Calling Ralph Ellison. Come in, Ralph. Come on in!") Larry Neal enjoined in "Any Day Now":

> Take the energy and the feeling of the blues, the mangled bodies, the broken marriages, the moaning nights, the shouting, the violence, the love cheating, the lonely sounding train whistles, and shape these into an art that stands for the spiritual helpmate of the Black nation. Make a form that uses the Soul Force of energy, and direct that form toward the liberation of Black people. (P. 161)

This still seems — even in the smug deconstructive days of the mid-1980s — like sagacious advice and sound aesthetics to me. But then, perhaps my positive response is a result of my own leanings toward those ancestral forces Neal so eloquently encapsulized as a "blues god." Surely the closing lines of the poem I wrote in response to his death suggest both a rhythmic African pantheon and that eternal return that keeps any legitimately Afro-American critic or theoretician sane. The title of the poem is "Toward Guinea: For Larry Neal, 1937–1981." It concludes:

> And now you have left . . .
>
> Tomorrow's dawn will find you moving
>   toward Guinea:
> Jamming again on African ground,
> A bright reunion
> Of ancestral sound.

A bright reunion, indeed. Larry Neal is an ancestor who taught us that vernacular sounds are the force that keeps us moving on in a New World of endless transitions — the energy that gives our criticism and theory the resonance of train whistles in the Alabama night. By the end of his life, Larry had become a veritable master of *the West,* but he always located his spiritual center among *the rest of us.* Like the stability of the community he served, he was himself a blues continuity ("someone to count on") in a world of changes.

 # VI

An Editor from Chicago: Reflections on the Work of Hoyt Fuller

The following essay speaks for itself. I need add only that Hoyt Fuller was, for me, the breath and finer spirit of the cultural energies that I am attempting to define. He was a man of the spirit — the mentor that so many of us had never known in the academy. Like Alain Locke, he was the spiritual father and foremost editor of the period spanning my own progression from the Black Aesthetic to a Blues Theory, to a Poetics of Afro-American Women's Writing. His death in 1983 marked, I believe, the end of an era, but not an end — as he would so joyfully have acknowledged — of the motion of a resilient Afro-American expressive cultural spirit that was the joy of his life.

 The Afro-American liberation struggle took a paradigmatic step forward in the later sixties, and an established middle class was scarcely prepared for the volatility, irreverence, and heady xenophobia of the new generation. When this black middle class was not busy condemning the impracticality of new black ideals, its spokesmen simply remained silent, or shook their heads in knowing agreement with white friends who asserted that black nationalism and black expression would soon vanish.

In the world of Afro-American expressive culture such standard bearers as J. Saunders Redding lamented the new generation's dedication to nationalist ideals.[1] Redding not only disparaged the notion of a Black Aesthetic in itself, but also labeled (in the manner of his white liberal compeers) the poetry, theater, and criticism of the emergent generation as an intellectually unsound discourse of "hate," a naive racism in reverse.

From the security of academic studies and holding the newly gained (by Black Aestheticians) attention of the white world, middle-class spokesmen ridiculed the urban poetry, arts organizations, and critical formulas produced by black men and women of the sixties.[2] Fortunately, the middle class also contained black men and women who recognized the necessity for change. These men and women realized that a nonacademic course in the arts was an incumbency of a new generation. In Chicago alone, three seminal figures of an established generation—George Kent, Gwendolyn Brooks, and Hoyt W. Fuller, the editor of *Negro Digest*— stepped forward and allied themselves with the black arts.[3] It is the work of Fuller that forms the subject of this essay.

Fuller's 1968 essay "Towards a Black Aesthetic" demonstrates how clearly he perceived the aims of a new movement in Afro-American expressive culture.[4] Invoking the Chicago example of the Organization of Black American Culture's Writers Workshop, the essay projects a vision of emergent writers creating in accordance with distinctively black criteria and being judged by criteria adduced by black critics. The Black Aesthetic comes to stand in Fuller's essay for a systematic project in the arts; a signal of revolutionary politics; and an ideal space for Afro-American intellectual *communitas*. The essay is homiletic; it rebukes old, racist orthodoxies and exhorts a new generation to evangelical efforts on behalf of a liberated black future. Its first article of faith is that a dedicated generation can produce (and adduce standards of judgment for) "artistic works . . . which reflect the special character and imperatives of black experience" (p. 9).

The phrase "special character and imperatives" roots Fuller's essay in the separatist field that conditioned Afro-American life and discourse during the late 1960s and early 1970s. It also connects his essay to political and psychological strategies preeminent in Afro-American intellectual history from its very beginnings.

Describing conditions of black life during post–World War I years, the historian David Levering Lewis asserts that white America's fundamental drive during these years was to "'put the nigger in his place' . . . to keep him out of the officer corps, out of labor unions and skilled jobs, out of the North and quaking for his very existence in the South—and out of politics everywhere."[5] Lewis suggests that the gross national pressure of exclusion in economics, politics, and the professions forced Afro-Americans to seek areas where proscriptions were less rigid. Art, expressive culture, and entertainment were, in fact, less exclusive areas of American endeavor.

Lewis's description of a social world that gave birth to the Harlem Renaissance calls to mind a picture of, say, a black fiddler during slavery. We can envision the slave "livelying-up" a grand white ball held in the Great House. Both Fuller's focus on black expressive distinctiveness and Lewis's characterization of the national scene in the 1920s imply, I believe, a necessarily privileged status for the *expressive realm* in Afro-American cultural discourse. For, to return to our slave musician, it would seem pointless for the fiddler to craft strategies for buying, voting, or blasting his way into the Great House. "Playing" his way inside, however—with all the connotations accompanying the invocation of *homo ludens*—has frequently and ironically been a matter of white American invitation.

Like their predecessors of the 1920s (and in the manner of slave fiddlers), Black Aestheticians of the sixties and seventies saw black expression as the principal area in which the "special character and imperatives of black experience" had always been developed, articulated, and analyzed. For the black expressive domain has produced stunning entrances into national life for blacks—even during the very bleakest moments of the race's entrapment in an economics of slavery.

Hoyt Fuller saw, as clearly as any person of his era, that the special power of black expression was, finally, a tangible power

Hoyt W. Fuller

of entrance to which our intellectual history has always gestured. Hoyt knew also that this power was only truly *black* power when it preserved and developed the unique imperatives of a sui generis cultural tradition. In our own time, the most powerful manifestations of black expressive uniqueness and its capacities of entrance have been provided by black women's writing.

If there has been a breach in stonily conservative walls of exclusion in our decade, it has certainly been created and populated by Afro-American women. Since Hoyt championed such generationally distinctive black writers as Nella Larsen, Paule Marshall, and Carolyn Rodgers, he would, perhaps, have welcomed current developments in black women's creativity and scholarship. Certainly he understood that black expressive culture is an area of ceaseless change, and he realized that no rigid and inflexible system of codification would suffice. (In "Towards a Black Aesthetic," he noted the elusiveness and resistance to codification of Afro-American style, and suggested that "black writers themselves are well aware of the possibility that what they seek is, after all, beyond codifying.") While no one could have predicted the strong force of black women in contemporary American expressive culture, many who shared a faith in the Black Aesthetic insisted that our unique Afro-American expressive style is as much a product of Phillis Wheatley, Sojourner Truth, and Sonia Sanchez as of Jupiter Hammon, Frederick Douglass, and Amiri Baraka.

Hoyt wrote a laudatory preface for Larsen's *Quicksand,* a novel that few had even heard of before its paperback release in the seventies. And he served as friend and mentor to Carolyn Rodgers, encouraging her efforts, publishing her first poems in *Black World,* and announcing in his introduction to her volume *Paper Soul:* "Carolyn Rodgers will be heard. She has the artist's gift and the artist's vision, and it is clear even now that her pathway leads to the far and beautiful country."

In the development of Afro-American women critics, there are doubtless any number of instances of Hoyt's fruitful assistance. (One thinks of essays by Carolyn Fowler, Andrea Rushing, Eugenia Collier, and Eleanor Traylor in *Black World* and *First World.*) But one of the more striking instances of his influence was conveyed in a recent conversation that I had with Mary Helen Washington, editor of *Black Eyed Susans* and *Midnight Birds.* Professor Washington said: "Hoyt was the person who gave me incentive to write. . . . He had everybody's books in his house . . . and loved to encourage people to read from their own work when they visited."

Washington, a critic *extraordinaire* of the expressive efforts of black women, went on to describe her last visit to Atlanta while Fuller was alive, recalling the gathering at his home of Sterling Brown, Ernest Gaines, herself, and Paule Marshall. The range represented by such an assembly, as anyone familiar with Afro-American intellectual history knows, is immense. And all who were present *respected* Hoyt. The irony (an almost tragic one) of Washington's story was that she had been invited to a local black Atlanta college for a conference on the Black Aesthetic. Fuller, who lived virtually a few blocks from the school, had not even been told of the conference.

Maybe it was Hoyt's thoroughgoing intellectualism — his openness to the myriad books and currents of our manifold lives and his receptiveness to distinctive virtues of all revelatory projects in the black arts — maybe it was his indisputable commitment to such an intellectualism that intimidated those who had Ph.D.'s and nothing more. His early championship of black women's concerns should surprise no one who knew the man's intense affinity for the whirlwind; he was always close to the eye/I/we-ness of black arts energies in America. His assistance in what might be considered a black feminism was, nonetheless, atypical.

For the traditional view of black creativity and communality during the sixties and seventies is reflected by Etheridge Knight's "For Black Poets Who Think of Suicide."

> Black Poets should live — not leap
> From steel bridges (Like the white boys do.
> Black Poets should *live* — not lay
> Their necks on railroad tracks (like the white boys do.
> Black Poets should seek — but not search too much
> In sweet dark caves, nor hunt for snipe
> Down psychic trails (like the white boys do.
> For Black Poets belong to Black People. Are
> The Flutes of Black Lovers. Are
> The Organs of Black Sorrows. Are
> The Trumpets of Black Warriors.
> Let All Black Poets die as trumpets.
> And be buried in the dust of marching feet.[6]

This projection of a dark rank and file trooping toward some ideal state aborning is stirringly bellicose. It is in harmony with the ardently revolutionary cadences of its era. It is also overwhelmingly male-aggressive. Today, the machismo of "Black Power Brotherhood" has yielded to a more sisterly expressivity, an expressivity globally acclaimed.

The global popularity of black women's writing does not mean that the power for which the Black Aesthetic quested during the sixties and seventies has been achieved. It simply means that Afro-American expressiveness is protean. Like a liminal trickster, it survives, grows, develops, fragments, and recombines. It shifts

genders and resonantly blends genres in its capacity to assume
myriad effective forms.

Hoyt knew the power of an expressivity capable of changing the
joke and slipping the yoke. The immemorial resourcefulness of
black expression and its alliance with what can be called "black-
entrance potentials" in the United States were central to his argu-
ments for a Black Aesthetic. He fully understood the implications
of the scene in Ralph Ellison's novel *Invisible Man* in which Dr.
Bledsoe, a black college president, demands of the protagonist:
Haven't we *lied* enough decent homes and drives for you to display to white trustees?[7] The protagonist responds that he has taken
Mr. Norton, a white trustee, to see the slums of black life because
the trustee ordered him to do so. Bledsoe thunders: "He *ordered*
you. Dammit, white folk are always giving orders, it's a habit with
them. . . . My God, boy! You're black and living in the South—
did you forget how to lie?"

As Sterling Brown and other eloquent spokespersons have
pointed out: In Afro-America, to tell at all, or to set forth what
the white literary theorist Stanley Fish calls "a standard story,"
is *to lie*.[8] Witness the following from Zora Neale Hurston's *Mules
and Men*.

> *Zora Hurston:* Ah come to collect some old stories and tales
> and Ah know y'all know a plenty of 'em and that's why Ah headed
> straight for home.
> *B. Moseley:* What you mean, Zora, them big old lies we tell
> when we're jus' sittin' around here on the store porch doin' nothin'?[9]

"Doing nothing," one asks, because "nothing is doing" in white
America for black folks? The therapeutic strategy when "nothing is doing" consists (for black folks) in both a store-porch communality and an expressively astute lying. The means of transcending a state in which nothing's doing is, in a word, spirit work
defined as a unique style of expression—defined, in Black Aesthetic days, as a resource called "soul."

Hoyt knew that all black men and women in the United States
who had their eyes fully open, their ears properly attuned, and

their minds adequately receptive would champion an expressive enterprise that allowed them to be and to celebrate their individual, dark-skinned selves. I believe he understood in his era, just as we do in ours, that denigrations of our resonant black expressive cultural spirit by conservative scholars or writers in the United States constitute predictable acts by men and women who strive to maintain old hegemonies and nothing more.

In our day, we further understand that a driving careerism can lead even homegrown American blacks to condemn womanist developments, theoretical assertions, and critical advances in the black expressive arena. One can only say of such careerists that they prove what committed black spokespersons have always known, i.e., literacy is not necessarily coextensive with liberation in the individual Afro-American life. For it has surely been among career-enamored and literate black men and women that our spirit work as it manifested itself in the Black Aesthetic, black literary theory, and Afro-American womanist creativity and criticism has received its most vociferous condemnation. But it is perhaps the case that those who have most fervidly condemned have not been even remotely in touch with the expressive-spiritual wellsprings of black culture.

"It's uh known fact," says Zora Neale Hurston's protagonist Janie in *Their Eyes Were Watching God,* "you got tuh *go* there tuh *know* there." If one has never felt him or herself to be uniquely and spiritually black in life and expression, then one has never even been on ancestral ground. And it is only by traveling such ground that one comes to empathize with and understand the aims and objectives of, say, a Black Aesthetic. Hoyt Fuller journeyed gladly on ancestral soil. *Journey to Africa* was both a title and an entitlement that belonged to him well before trips to the "Motherland" became fashionable. Hoyt's spiritual legacy as an advocate for the Black Aesthetic and other progressive movements of the Afro-American expressive tradition stands in a relationship of identity with the most exalted dimensions of our intellectual history.

His signal role, of course, was that of editor of *Negro Digest, Black World,* and *First World* — journals in which he put many of us into print, bolstering our confidence and reassuring us that there were viable alternatives to the dreary world of standard American academic "scholarship." But Hoyt's contribution to our collective life went far beyond his position as an editor. The characterization of Maxwell Perkins (the editor who discovered and exerted such influence on the works of Fitzgerald, Hemingway, Caldwell, and others) rendered by Thomas Wolfe captures the feeling that many of us had for Hoyt.

Wolfe's *Of Time and the River* is dedicated to "A great editor and a brave and honest man, who stuck to the writer of this book through times of bitter hopelessness and doubt and would not let him give in to his own despair." What better conclusion can there be for reflections on Hoyt Fuller than the assertion that he was a great editor, a brave and honest man, and an unflinching friend. His legacy, finally, is the dramatic motion forward of the black expressive spirit that he resolutely championed during the past two decades of our collective cultural life in America.

Conclusion

In the 60's there was enough feeling enough emotion to go round.
There was no reason to be square, that's what we felt. We could
do anything, be anything, even free. That's how young we were.
That's now long ago, that was.

— Amiri Baraka, "Courageousness"

 There are few moralists who don't discover in their
own lives indisputable evidence of their own unim-
peachable morality. Similarly, there are few critics who
do not find in their own work evidence of their own stunning
fidelity to the "spirit" of their subject. Neither the moralist nor
the critic, however, is likely to see his or her evaluations as self-
congratulatory. Both usually feel that they have proposed general
or universal principles which, upon careful self-examination, they
find reflected in the particulars of their own lives. Governed by
standards of a general virtue or a universalist objectivity, neither
the moralist nor the critic wishes to acknowledge the determinacy
of language, vested interests, privileged interpretive postures, or
a will to power in the domains of value and evaluation.

At least since Samuel Coleridge's reservations in his *Biographia*
about the merely idiosyncratic features of William Wordsworth's
verse — or perhaps it is at least since Socrates set the ideal vision
of the state against the idiosyncratic and merely personal reveries
of the poets — moralists, poets, and critics have been cautioned
against the personal. We listen for a brief moment to T. S. Eliot:

"One error, in fact, of eccentricity in poetry is to seek for new human emotions to express; and in this search for novelty in the wrong place it discovers the perverse. . . . Poetry is not a turning loose of emotion, but an escape from emotion; it is not the expression of personality, but an escape from personality."[1] Eliot not only brings the classical argument home with full force but also states precisely the criteria by which my foregoing discussions are disqualified as standard poetry and, perhaps, aptly characterized as "perverse." But before rushing to this judgment, let's pause for a moment, descending carefully from the lofty heights of moralism and classical criticism to speak person to person— even off the record.

Critics follow, always, a purely personal line. In their most self-aware moments they have no doubt whatsoever about the specifiable determinants of every one of their favorite essays, reviews, lectures, and pedagogical utterances.

Now if a critic chooses never to be "personal," that simply means that he or she has made an entirely personal choice. Who, after all, in our most self-directing moments stands over us, saying, "Now, Houston, you'll probably want to perform a search-and-replace operation when you're finished, changing all of your 'I's' to 'ones' "? There are, to be sure, institutional conventions, career and market constraints, that serve as implicit censors for us all. But, finally, we make our own choices and are seldom deceived, I think, about the "personal" determinacy of our work. The search-and-replace operation that forestalls recognition (sometimes even self-recognition) of the personal is the substitution of *human* or *universal* values for what actually operates any given critic's enterprise—*my* values.

The substitution is always in the service of powerful interests (one's own included) that seek to maintain the status quo in the name of the general, the universal, or *la condition humaine*. But as a critic normally works—even under such rigorously political circumstances as those of, say, Mikhail Bakhtin—the *condition* closest at hand is his or her very personal one.

For a critic, then, to acknowledge autobiography as a driving genre of criticism is for him or her to do no more than tell the truth. When I "analyze," for you my reader, a poem or a novel,

I am merely offering you—under the conventions of criticism, a peculiar and covering style, as it were—a determinate recall of my experiences. This is not to plump down squarely for a return to journeys of sensitive souls among the masterpieces. Both "sensitive" nd "masterpieces" were overdetermined in that form of impressionism. No, what "recall" implies here is a narrative, which begins, as Barbara Herrnstein Smith argues in *On the Margins of Discourse,* with the founding condition "something happened."[2] My critical position is a personal condition marked by the narration of what happened, *to me.* And, yes, this does sound like one of the eternal returns that mark a life's journey. For the decisive emphasis (mine) on "to me" resurrects the British aestheticism of my early days.

Walter Pater in *The Renaissance* exquisitely says that an Arnoldian injunction to see *the* object "as in itself it really is" demands a qualified restatement. For Pater, the aim was to see *a* particular, unique object as it is, *to me.* I am not, finally, advocating more than an autobiographical allowance in our descriptive catalogue of *the* critic—an allowance that transforms both him or her and his or her practice into *a* critic—a very particularly accounted-for expressive product and experience. Such an allowance opens, I feel, a space for what I call *personal poetry* in the critical field.[3]

Stated directly in terms of my current critical practice, an autobiographical allowance enables racial poetry to displace state philosophy. Autobiography and phenomenology are then free to converge under the condition of *Poetics.* In a sense approved by Gaston Bachelard, *poetics* can be defined as the emergence of a poetic image (visual, tactile, or auditory) that displaces the causal explanations of investigative "sciences" such as psychology or psychoanalysis.[4] Poetics is a meditative enterprise that privileges the poetic image, or the unique expressive *sound* of a culture, as the founding or generative force of the culture. Such forces are held, in my reading of Bachelard, to be creatively spiritual and underdetermined. And for me, the very ability to move to an Afro-American poetics requires an autobiographical recall of the auditory.

I myself had to leave behind universal, objective, and standard causal models that mark a normal practice of literary criticism in the United States. In order to compose the present book, I had to put the standard on hold in order to talk and listen to voices from low and signifying grounds of my own Afro-American expressive culture.

This book, as I have stated earlier, is a middle passage. Having questioned, in sharp ways, the normal practice of Afro-American literary criticism in *Modernism and the Harlem Renaissance,* I felt compelled to give, in the most interesting manner possible, both an account and exemplification of my own relationship to standard critical practices. What I hope will prove most exemplary in the present book, however, are not the limitations of previously published essays but their racial or expressive cultural virtues found, suggested, or invented in my revisions and refigurations. Further exemplary and, I hope, empowering are my attempts honestly to indicate the delusions, traps, pitfalls, arrogance, misjudgments, and other shortcomings that have marked my journey from the provinces of a New Criticism of British Victorian literature to an Afro-American Blues Criticism. In the final book of my trilogy, *Workings of the Spirit,* I further advocate a sui generis poetics. Only an account of what happened "way down yonder by myself" delivered as *personalist* criticism has enabled me to avoid Santayana's dreaded fate of reliving, rather than revising.

Moreover, it is probably only in my autobiographical moments that I have been compelled, despite myself, to honesty. And here I come to final qualifications, revisions, and ratios for the Black Arts era that was so significant for my critical progress.

If my own critical motion has been a kind of enactment of Afro-American spirit motion, it has, nonetheless, both suffered and perpetuated the various excesses, misunderstandings, and mistakes that mark any given or fixed position. Looking back, then, as I am going to do forthwith, at the Black Arts through *The Autobiography of LeRoi Jones Amiri Baraka* is as much a self-naming as anything else.[5] I was as infatuated as most of my cohorts by the workings of "power" that I shall attempt to characterize.

Having grown up in a Kentucky where almost all who carried guns, wore uniforms, and had the authority to shatter my life with a word or a bullet were white, I was ecstatic at the emergence of black men and women in black berets, leather jackets, and other components of the Black Panther uniform. I was happy to see those who wore such uniforms "taking up the gun." Theirs was a redaction of white racism that I found liberating.

And the words, the rhetoric, the "We don't love you" authority of Black Power language was more than captivating. It was utterly enthralling. And I delighted in turning this language against perceived white enemies any and everywhere. There is an image implicit here of the critic as "Mau Mauer."

What an ironically disgusting place to return to, I now think, remembering those white-uniformed gun-toters who delighted in calling us "Little niggers" and pulling us over for "inspection" in the city of my youth.

I was sometimes bombastic during my Black Aesthetic days, sometimes aggressively insulting to white people who had no access to my life in the United States and who merely wanted information. In my uniformed moments, I am sure that I sometimes did little good for spirit work, other people, the cause of criticism, or myself. I regret those moments and offer a much belated apology to people of goodwill who received bullet words rather than finer resonances of an Afro-American spirit.

How, today, can one understand the bullet talk of our recent past except by scrutinizing its dynamics? A backward glance is the answer, a revision of very recently traveled roads.

What first emerges from such a backward glance is an image of a publicly enthusiastic group of culture workers awaiting a rebirth of wonder. Behind the public facade, utterances, and idealism of those of us who occupied the sixties, however, there often lurked myriad evils that only The Shadow comprehended as common stock in the hearts of men, and women. My reference to the adventure-story hero is, of course, intentional, carrying me immediately to *The Autobiography of LeRoi Jones Amiri Baraka*. As I recently read this work, I was struck by how profoundly influenced and captivated by heroes such as The Shadow Baraka has always been. He has been continuously dedicated, I now feel, to a kind of serio-comic adventurism that only such heroes can persuasively sustain. Each phase of his protean career has been marked by a "secret," romanticized, paramilitary group of associates dedicated, as far as I can discern, to what Baraka calls "Afro-American Street Therapy, a good ass-kicking" (p. 206).

The pattern of Baraka's life seems to move the self from bellicose childhood gangs like the "Secret Seven" to middle-age Green Lantern "woofin" — with jaunts in a romantically conceived, but realistically horrible, "Error Farce" (Air Force) and white bohemia as bridges. From this morass of adventurism, I unearthed the key to the collapse of the Harlem Black Arts Repertory Theatre School.

Baraka claims, in his autobiography, to be puzzled about his own refusal in the sixties to expunge a bullying and criminal contingent from the school. Though he knew that the contingent represented by Shammy and Tong Hackensack (pseudonyms, of course) would bring about the downfall of the Black Arts, he refused to act: "Finally, there were more people wanting to kick the two Hackensack brothers' asses than you could kill with a submachine gun without a lot of extra clips. They were a major problem at the Arts" (p. 206). A "major problem," indeed, since Baraka calls Tong "the maddest goddam nut I'd ever met" (p. 209).

After a reading of the whole of Baraka's autobiography, there is little mystery about the failure of the founder of the Black Arts to purge the madmen. A recalled adolescent incident leads the way to understanding. When two men accost Baraka at a fast food establishment and one of them (the biggest, of course) accuses the young LeRoi Jones of thinking he is "tough," Jones/Baraka pokes out his chin (adventure-story style) and says: "I am tough!" Laughter and the friendship of the toughs follow. Baraka did not purge the Hackensacks from the Black Arts because he considered himself — at heart (and in the streets and beds of bohemia) — a tough guy.

This is a "hard fact," but it is one that should be examined for any fit judgment of the sixties. From Baraka's autobiography we learn of an addicted Ron Karenga slurring threats at the poet on the telephone while just inside Karenga's door sits a mounted machine gun, awaiting, presumably, the attack of men with "evil" in their hearts. We read of Baraka himself sexually exploiting a teenager, deserting his wife and children, and scheming to move two women into his building so that he can exploit them in the name of "African polygamy."

In *private,* Baraka, who was a foremost public advocate for the Black Arts is: The Artist as Thug. The tough guy stands in seamy opposition to the idealistic, revolutionary culture worker. The criminal and asocial private aspects of the sixties could, perhaps, be held in abeyance. But such a suppression would prevent us from arriving at that second sign in an American equation called "Black Power." Having reread the twenties under the sign of blackness or race, it is now incumbent to read the sixties under the sign "power."

While the twenties seem to have found their way profitably to the lowground and inaudible valleys of "race" (some willy-nilly, some in spite of themselves), participants in the Black Arts often failed, I believe, to negotiate the intricacies of "power." Principal confusions of Black Arts workers and critics — myself included — involved a failure to distinguish between bullying militarism and revolutionary organization, between cults and interest groups, between religious chicanery and nationalist politics, and, finally, between verbal throwaways designed for political rallies and carefully articulated Afro-American expressive texts. Bullet words and paramilitary posturing were read as signs of black "power," and a rhetoric of hard facts was mistaken for a realization of genuine expressive power.

The white academy and the white creative and critical establishment of America helped, profitably, to perpetuate such failures by advancing hastily conceived poverty, black studies, housing, and minority small business *programs.* Money was available for a "war on poverty," a sort of tossed-off treasure chest to keep black folks running. And black folks did respond.

"TAKE THE MONEY AND RUN" was not only the injunction of black urban rebellions but also the attitude of many blacks empowered to supervise programs intended to quell such rebellions. Power became equated with Yankee dollars.

In the Black Arts, loudspeaking resulted in a plethora of drum-like, monotonous, and sometimes silly utterances passed off as the "New Black Poetry." Black critical complicity emerged as a Black Aesthetic which sometimes proclaimed: "If it's too loud, you're too old!" Which is to say, anyone (especially *white* ones) who had reservations, questions, or criticisms was deemed too pedantic, bourgeois, or unrevolutionary to comprehend the excellence of *all* black works.

I surely must seem uncharitable in this assessment. For, as I have acknowledged, the sixties gave birth to me as an "Afro-American" and as an Afro-American critic. I believe the present assessment is necessary, though, as a release and relief of the spirit.

But why is it that we need a release? Because nostalgia is a form of arrested development akin to hero worship. It tends to construct idealized landscapes and portraits. And it is almost always too self-exonerating. The nostalgic voice may say: "Ah, but I was young and naive and too easily persuaded by others." But it will seldom proclaim: "I was a bullying, sometimes petulant, artist-as-thug." It is likewise reluctant to admit that dashikis and long hair and bullet words were frequently gestures of ignorance and a thuggish will to power. It is best, then, to take the filter off the lenses, to raise the scrim and catch a realistic vision of what was up in the sixties. Yes . . . but still there remains a challenge: "What's up with *that?*"

I mean, where do I, or where does anyone else, derive the privilege of decrying aggressive, thuggish, militaristic behavior, or other drawbacks of the sixties? To assume such a privilege is, perhaps, to imply that all aggression is evil and anomalous for Afro-America. It may also be to propose a harmonious, largely passive, beatific, and well-scrubbed congregation of easy churchgoers as the cast that would more profitably have occupied the sixties — or any other era of Afro-American life.

The birth of Afro-America as a physical enterprise — a real country in the known world — began, however, with the most thuggish, violent, and degraded architects of all — European males who financed, oversaw, and ran a holocaustal Atlantic slave trade. Eric Williams' *Capitalism and Slavery* dispels, with brilliant persuasiveness, any notion that the trade was sustained for reasons other than profit.[6] The trade combined thuggery and avariciousness in horrendous workings of "power" that shattered fifty to one hundred *million* African lives.

The power equations of the Atlantic slave trade wrote themselves, in recent decades, as an outgoing white violence against black men, women, and children who nonviolently asked, marched, and prayed for rights that the Constitution and laws of the United States said belonged to them. Emmett Till, Medgar Evers, Malcolm X, Martin Luther King, Jr., four young black girls in a Birmingham church – all murdered – were martyrs to white American thuggery par excellence.

Nine children in Little Rock, Arkansas – the best and brightest of their black high school classes – surrounded by southern white mobs shouting "Niggers go home," and one of the nine recalling years later: "It got so bad, we thought we'd have to let them have one of the children to hang so the other eight could get away." White Hollywood, Madison Avenue, Broadway were all doing a brisk business in "blackness" during such horrors. "Disaster," says the persona of one African poet's satire, "tell me about disaster."

Racist offensives, however, have never been simply "suffered" by black people. Frederick Douglass's meditations on the spirit motion represented by a determination to learn how to read in his *Narrative* are complemented by his recounting of the process by which "a slave was made a man."[7] This process of identity making, as Douglass describes it, is a nineteenth-century rendition of "Afro-American Street Therapy." Douglass whips the behinds of those who would be complicitous with the slavebreaker *and* of Mr. Covey the slavebreaker himself. If you intend to stop being whipped by white thugs, Douglass suggests, you have to do a little therapy and speak bullet words: "I felt as I never felt before [after standing off Covey]. It was a glorious resurrection, from the tomb of slavery, to the heaven of freedom. My long-crushed spirit rose . . . I did not hesitate to let it be known of me, that the white man who expected to succeed in whipping, must also succeed in killing me" (p. 113).

I have indicated the seamier sides, the thuggish and nonhumanistic sides of Afro-American aggressive resistance during the sixties. On the more positive side of such resistance is the actual empowerment that it provided. It is indisputably the case that had there been no aggressive Black Power offensive during the late sixties and early seventies, whites surely would have felt free to continue to whip black heads and to kill black leaders on prime-time television. The entrance of the "tough guys" changed all of that.

At Yale, for example, the president and his men became aggressively willing to talk to black "intellectuals" after the Black Panther party organized in New Haven. Malcolm X, with his usual perspicacity, realized years ago that when he emerged as a militant and charismatic national black leader, white people were suddenly eager to hear the integrationist rhetoric of Martin Luther King.

The doors of business, the academy, and the professions opened more as a direct function of Afro-American street therapy than as a response to beneficent changes of white American hearts. Spirit motion, therefore, as I define it, includes an active will to resistance. In *Black Boy,* Richard Wright's narrator expresses such progressive, active, and resistant motion in the words "I've got to get away; I can't stay here."[8]

Like Wright's narrator, Afro-American expressive artists have never accepted any single place or restrictive definition of their moving spirit. From Black Arts in the sixties we have moved therefore to a splendid outpouring of Afro-American women's writing in the eighties. Such writing is currently the most resonant manifestation of Afro-American spirit work in the United States. A critic committed to such work has no choice but to follow its currents to a poetics of Afro-American women's writing.

Such, in any case, is the interpretation of contemporary Afro-American creativity that seems most tenable — to me.

Notes & Index

Notes

Introduction

1. Houston A. Baker, Jr., *Modernism and the Harlem Renaissance* (Chicago: University of Chicago Press, 1987).

2. Houston A. Baker, Jr., *Workings of the Spirit: The Poetics of Afro-American Women's Writing* (Chicago: University of Chicago Press, in press).

3. The producer of the controversial film *Birth of a Nation* which was boycotted and picketed by Afro-Americans on its release during the second decade of our century.

4. Jean Toomer, *Cane* (New York: Liveright, 1975).

5. The work of Hayden White in *Metahistory, Tropics of Discourse,* and *The Content of the Form* is essential in the conceptualization of historical *emplotment.*

6. Nathan Irvin Huggins, *Harlem Renaissance* (New York: Oxford, 1971). David Levering Lewis, *When Harlem Was in Vogue* (New York: Knopf, 1981).

7. The lines belong to Run—DMC's *Raising Hell* album.

Chapter I: Journey toward Black Art

1. William Stanley Braithwaite, "The Negro in American Literature," in *The New Negro,* ed. Alain Locke (New York: Atheneum, 1968), pp. 29-44.

2. Langston Hughes, "The Negro Artist and the Racial Mountain," *Amistad I* (New York: Random House, 1970), pp. 301-5. (First published in the *Nation,* June 23, 1926.)

3. Thurman lived a flamboyant life in New York and Hollywood from 1925 to 1934. He died of alcoholism and tuberculosis on New York's Welfare Island. For a brief biographical sketch, see Dorothy West's "Elephant Dance," *Black World* 20 (November 1970): 77-85.

4. Claude McKay, *A Long Way from Home* (New York: Harcourt, Brace and World, 1970). McKay's autobiography describes his travels during the twenties and contains his reflections on the Harlem Renaissance.

5. For accounts of the Harlem Renaissance in general and the careers of Cullen and Hughes during the twenties, see Langston Hughes's *The Big Sea* (New York: Hill and Wang, 1968) and Blanche E. Ferguson's *Countee Cullen and the Negro Renaissance* (New York: Dodd, Mead, 1966). Hughes's autobiography was first published in 1940.

6. Arna Bontemps, Introduction to Jean Toomer, *Cane* (New York: Harper and Row, 1969), p. x.

7. Jean Toomer, *Cane* (New York: Harper and Row, 1969), p. 1. All citations of *Cane* in my text refer to this edition.

8. I am indebted to Professor James Nash for his suggestion concerning duality in *Cane,* and I cannot thank him enough for reading my manuscript and contributing his editorial skills toward its completion.

9. William J. Goede, "Jean Toomer's Ralph Kabnis: Portrait of the Negro Artist as a Young Man," *Phylon* 30 (1969): 75. In *The Negro Novel in America* (New Haven: Yale University Press, 1965), Robert Bone calls Becky's house "a cabin built by community guilt" (p. 83).

10. Georges Devereux, *Essais d'ethnopsychiatric générale,* trans. Henri Gobard (Paris: Gallimard, 1970), p. 18. An entire section of Devereux's first chapter (pp. 14–31) is devoted to what he terms *les désordres sacrés (chamaniques),* and I wish to thank Mme. Yvette Rude of the University of Paris-Vincennes for calling my attention to the work.

11. Bontemps, Introduction, pp. xii–xiii.

12. Quoted by Alain Locke in "Negro Youth Speaks," *New Negro,* p. 51.

13. In "The Aggregate Man in Jean Toomer's *Cane,*" *Studies in the Novel* 3 (1971): 190–213, William C. Fischer says: "The moving force behind the abuse and pain endured by Toomer's women is in fact the relentless debilitation of the black man in the white rural South."

14. For a further discussion of this theme and its ramifications, see my essay "Freedom and Apocalypse: A Thematic Approach to Black Expression," *Long Black Song: Essays in Black American Literature and Culture* (Charlottesville: University Press of Virginia, 1972), pp. 42–57.

15. Edward E. Waldron, "The Search for Identity in Jean Toomer's 'Esther,'" *CLA Journal* 14 (1971): 277.

16. A professional individual for whom Toomer had great aversion: "There seems to have been no shopkeepers or shysters among us," he said in his letter to the editors of the *Liberator* in 1922 (quoted from Bontemps, Introduction, p. ix). In "Kabnis," there appears not only the

unfavorable portrayal of the businessman Halsey but also the protagonist's bitterly cynical denunciation: "Hence, what comes from Him is ugly. Lynchers and business men, and that cockroach Hanby, especially" (p. 162).

17. Fischer, "Aggregate Man in Jean Toomer's *Cane*," p. 200.

18. In David Walker's *Appeal* (1829), Frederick Douglass's *Narrative of the Life of Frederick Douglass* (1845), and William Wells Brown's *Narrative of William Wells Brown, A Fugitive Slave* (1847), there are innumerable passages condemning supposedly Christian whites who enslave and brutalize black Americans.

19. In "Jean Toomer's Black Authenticity," *Black World* 20 (1970): 70–76, Clifford Mason comments aptly that Toomer realized that "the emptiness of our black lives has been due as much to our being psychological mimics as it has been to the accumulation of what the white man has wrought."

20. James Edwin Howard takes this same line of analysis in his "Structure and Search in Jean Toomer's *Cane*" (typescript, University of Virginia, 1970), p. 3.

21. Goede, "Jean Toomer's Ralph Kabnis."

22. Darwin T. Turner, "Jean Toomer's *Cane*," *Negro Digest* 18 (January 1969): 5.

23. Bone, *Negro Novel in America*, p. 84.

24. Imamu Amiri Baraka [LeRoi Jones], "The Dance," *The Dead Lecturer* (New York: Grove, 1964), p. 71.

25. Bone, Fischer, and Turner all see the protagonist of "Kabnis" as a failure in his quest for meaning. And in "A Key to the Poems in *Cane*," *CLA Journal* 14 (March 1971): 251–58, Bernard Bell describes him in the same terms.

26. Bontemps, Introduction, p. xiii.

27. Goede, "Jean Toomer's Ralph Kabnis," p. 85.

28. Eugenia W. Collier, "Heritage from Harlem," *Black World* 20 (November 1970): 54. For further discussion of the folk influence during the Harlem Renaissance, see the introduction to "The Awakening of the Twenties" and "Black American Literature: An Overview" in my *Black Literature in America* (New York: McGraw-Hill, 1971).

Chapter II: A Many-Colored Coat of Dreams

1. Stephen H. Bronz, *Roots of Negro Racial Consciousness* (New York: Libra, 1964), pp. 64–65.

2. Countee Cullen, ed., *Caroling Dusk* (New York: Harper and Row, 1927), p. 179. All citations from *Caroling Dusk* in my text refer to this edition.

3. James Weldon Johnson, *Along This Way* (New York: Viking, 1968), p. 160.

4. Arna Bontemps, "The Negro Contribution to American Letters," in *The American Negro Reference Book* (Englewood Cliffs, N.J.: Prentice-Hall, 1966), pp. 854–55.

5. W. E. B. DuBois, "Criteria of Negro Art," *Crisis* 32 (1926):296.

6. Darwin T. Turner, "Countee Cullen: The Lost Ariel," *In a Minor Chord* (Carbondale: Southern Illinois University Press, 1971), pp. 60–88. Turner follows the lead of J. Saunders Redding, who called Cullen "the Ariel of Negro poets" in *To Make a Poet Black* (Chapel Hill: University of North Carolina Press, 1939), p. 111.

7. Nathan Irvin Huggins, *Harlem Renaissance* (New York: Oxford, 1971), p. 206.

8. Fred Beauford, "A Conversation with Ishmael Reed," *Black Creation* 4 (1973):13. The description is Reed's.

9. Blanche E. Ferguson, *Countee Cullen and the Negro Renaissance* (New York: Dodd, Mead, 1966), p. 41. This is currently the most complete published biography of Cullen, and I have relied heavily upon it for the information contained in my brief overview of the poet's life.

10. Arna Bontemps, "The Harlem Renaissance," *Saturday Review* 30 (1947):12.

11. Langston Hughes, *The Big Sea* (New York: Hill and Wang, 1963), pp. 311–30.

12. An interview with Marjorie Content Toomer conducted by Ann Allen Shockley for the Fisk University Black Oral History Program, Special Collections, Fisk University Library, Nashville, Tenn.

13. In *Harlem Renaissance*, Nathan Huggins says: "It was Cullen who told Langston Hughes that he wanted to be a poet, not a Negro poet" (p. 208). The author is referring to Hughes's introductory remarks in "The Negro Artist and the Racial Mountain," in *The Black Aesthetic*, ed. Addison Gayle, Jr. (New York: Doubleday, 1971). Hughes calls no names; Huggins lists one without a footnote.

14. W. E. B. DuBois, "Our Book Shelf," *Crisis* 31 (1926):239.

15. Alain Locke, "Negro Youth Speaks," in *The New Negro*, ed. Alain Locke (New York: Atheneum, 1968), p. 52.

16. James Weldon Johnson, ed., *The Book of American Negro Poetry* (New York: Harcourt, Brace & World, 1959), pp. 219–20.

17. Countee Cullen, "The Negro in Art," *Crisis* 32 (1926):193.

18. Quoted from Turner, "Countee Cullen," pp. 77–78.

19. Countee Cullen, "Countee Cullen on Miscegenation," *Crisis* 34 (1929):373.

20. Cullen, "Negro in Art," p. 194.

21. Cullen, *Caroling Dusk,* p. xii.

22. Countee Cullen, "The Dark Tower," *Opportunity* 5 (1927):180.

23. Cullen, *Caroling Dusk,* p. 180.

24. Quoted from Bronz, *Roots of Negro Racial Consciousness,* p. 58.

25. Quoted from Beulah Reimherr, "Race Consciousness in Countee Cullen's Poetry," *Susquehanna University Studies* 7 (1963):67.

26. Cullen, "Negro in Art," p. 193.

27. Bontemps, "Harlem Renaissance," p. 44.

28. Johnson, *Book of American Negro Poetry,* p. 39.

29. Cullen, *Caroling Dusk,* p. 179.

30. Countee Cullen, "To You Who Read My Book," *Color* (New York: Harper and Bros., 1925). All citations from *Color* in my text refer to this edition. In this and the following discussions, I have omitted line and page references: the reader can locate most of the quoted passages easily.

31. Bertram L. Woodruff, "The Poetic Philosophy of Countee Cullen," *Phylon* 1 (1940):213–23.

32. Johnson, *Book of American Negro Poetry,* p. 221.

33. Arthur P. Davis, "The Alien-and-Exile Theme in Countee Cullen's Racial Poems," *Phylon* 14 (1953):390.

34. The charges come from Bronz, *Roots of Negro Racial Consciousness,* and Turner, "Countee Cullen," respectively.

35. In "Major Themes in the Poetry of Countee Cullen," in *The Harlem Renaissance Remembered,* ed. Arna Bontemps (New York: Dodd, Mead, 1972), pp. 115–18, Nicholas Canaday points out that both "Incident" and the later "Uncle Jim" are poems of initiation.

36. Ibid., pp. 104–6. Canaday offers a good discussion of Cullen's pervasive use of religious imagery and forms.

37. Johnson, *Along This Way,* p. 161.

38. Benjamin Brawley, *The Negro Genius* (New York: Dodd, Mead, 1937), p. 226.

39. Countee Cullen, *Copper Sun* (New York: Harper and Bros., 1927). All citations from *Copper Sun* in my text refer to this edition.

40. W. K. Wimsatt, *The Verbal Icon: Studies in the Meaning of Poetry* (Lexington: University of Kentucky Press, 1954).

41. Harvey Curtis Webster, "A Difficult Career," *Poetry* 70 (1947):224.

42. Countee Cullen, "The Ballad of the Brown Girl, An Old Ballad Retold," *On These I Stand* (New York: Harper and Row, 1947), pp. 175-82. All citations from *The Ballad of the Brown Girl* in my text refer to this version.

43. Countee Cullen, *The Black Christ and Other Poems* (New York: Harper and Bros., 1929). All citations from *The Black Christ* in my text refer to this edition.

44. Countee Cullen, *The Medea and Some Poems* (New York: Harper and Bros., 1935). All citations from *The Medea* in my text refer to this edition.

45. John Keats to Benjamin Bailey, January 3, 1818, in John Keats, *Selected Poems and Letters,* ed. Douglas Bush (Boston: Houghton Mifflin, 1959), p. 262.

Chapter III: Lowground and Inaudible Valleys

1. "To Maecenas," *The Poems of Phillis Wheatley,* ed. Julian D. Mason, Jr. (Chapel Hill: University of North Carolina Press, 1966), p. 4.

2. John A. Williams, *The Man Who Cried I Am* (New York: Signet, 1967).

3. I use the phrase here after the manner of Vincent Harding's lyrical and passionate history of the black struggle for freedom in America, *There Is a River* (New York: Harcourt, 1981): "At first, as the river metaphor took life within me, I was unduly concerned about its apparent inexactness and ambiguity. Now, with the passing of time and the deepening of our vision, it is possible to recognize that we are indeed the river, and at the same time that the river is more than us—generations more, millions more. Through such an opening we may sense that the river of black struggle is people, but it is also the hope, the movement, the transformative power that humans create and that create them, us, and makes them, us, new persons. So we black people are the river; the river is us" (p. xix).

4. The paraphrase comes from Wheatstraw's "Road Tramp Blues," which begin, "I am what I am and all I was born to be."

5. LeRoi Jones, *Target Study,* poems written from 1963 to 1965, and included in the volume *Black Magic: Poetry, 1961-1967* (Indianapolis: Bobbs-Merrill, 1969), p. 55.

6. My sources here include statistics quoted freely on a recent television program hosted by Bill Moyers and called "The Crisis of the Black Family." There is also the recent series of articles published by the *Washington Post* in which Professors Joyce Ladner and Harriet

McAdoo — two black scholars — serve as experts detailing the collapse of the black family and the feminization of poverty.

7. Henry Louis Gates, Jr., "Preface to Blackness: Text and Pretext," in *Afro-American Literature: The Reconstruction of Instruction,* eds. Robert Stepto and Dexter Fisher (New York: Modern Language Association, 1978).

8. Alan Shucard, *Countee Cullen* (Detroit: Twayne, 1985).

9. In *Modernism and the Harlem Renaissance* (Chicago, 1987). In that work, I seek to define a black "discursive field" that has always *sounded* in America.

10. The title is that of a study subtitled *A Study of the Performed African-American Sermon,* by Gerald L. Davis (Philadelphia: University of Pennsylvania Press, 1985).

11. These are lines from a traditional Afro-American spiritual, "I Couldn't Hear Nobody Pray."

12. Nellie McKay, *Jean Toomer, Artist* (Chapel Hill: University of North Carolina Press, 1984).

13. McKay (ibid., p. 243) writes of Toomer's labors on *Cane* as follows: "While he worked on the book, Toomer's deep mysticism and intent search for spiritual connections made the experience almost supernatural. The essence of black culture enveloped and filled him. He even wrote to Waldo Frank describing times when he felt that he was losing all sense of an identity separate from the materials of his writing." I shall discuss Toomer's mystical dissolving of personality in a moment.

14. Jean Toomer, *Cane* (New York: Liveright, 1975). All citations refer to this edition, which contains an introduction by Darwin Turner.

15. Two sources have been useful to me in reviewing research on trance and coming to some understanding of the phenomenon's complexity: John Curtis Gowen, *Trance, Art, and Creativity* (Buffalo, N.Y.: Creative Education Foundation, 1975); Jane Belo, *Trance in Bali* (New York: Columbia University Press, 1960).

16. Belo, *Trance in Bali.*

17. Susan Sontag, "The Aesthetics of Silence," *A Susan Sontag Reader* (New York: Vintage, 1983), pp. 181–204. All citations refer to this edition.

18. In Lance Jeffers, "My Blackness Is the Beauty of This Land," the title poem of the poet's first volume (Detroit: Broadside Press, 1970), p. 9. "While I here standing black beside / wrench tears from with the lies would suck the salt / to make me more American than America. . . . / But yet my love and yet my hate shall civilize this land, / this land's salvation."

19. *Paris Review* 101 (1986), p. 203. Walcott goes on in the interview to speak of the trancelike state which makes a silent space for a poem's creation.

Chapter IV: "These Are Songs If You Have the / Music"

1. William Mahoney, "Travels in the South: A Cold Night in Alabama," in *Black Fire,* eds. LeRoi Jones and Larry Neal (New York: William Morrow, 1968), pp. 144-48.
2. Ibid., pp. 146-47.
3. LeRoi Jones, *Preface to a Twenty-Volume Suicide Note* (New York: Totem Press and Corinth Books, 1961).
4. LeRoi Jones, *Home, Social Essays* (New York: William Morrow, 1966).
5. LeRoi Jones, *Dutchman* and *The Slave* (New York: William Morrow, 1964).
6. LeRoi Jones, *Target Study,* in *Black Magic: Poetry, 1961-1967* (Indianapolis: Bobbs-Merrill, 1969). *Black Magic* contains three groups of poems. Besides *Target Study,* which includes poems written between 1963 and 1965, there are *Sabotage* (1961-63) and *Black Art* (1965-66).
7. LeRoi Jones, *The Dead Lecturer* (New York: Grove, 1964).
8. LeRoi Jones, *Four Black Revolutionary Plays* (Indianapolis: Bobbs-Merrill, 1969).
9. LeRoi Jones, *Tales* (New York: Grove, 1967).
10. LeRoi Jones, *The System of Dante's Hell* (New York: Grove, 1966). I am, of course, aware that Baraka speaks of his novel as reflecting his vision of the years 1960-61. I also realize that some stories in *Tales* appeared earlier than 1967. Two chapters from the novel appear in Herbert Hill's controversial anthology *Soon, One Morning* (1963). Baraka did not arrive at the "collected" vision for either work, however, until he prepared them for publication. It seems logical, therefore, to move in accord with the publication dates.
11. Ralph Ellison, *Shadow and Act* (New York: Signet, 1966), p. 90.
12. Imamu Amiri Baraka, *Raise, Race, Rays, Raze: Essays since 1965* (New York: Vintage, 1972).
13. Imamu Amiri Baraka, *Spirit Reach* (Newark: Jihad Productions, 1972). I have chosen to neglect Baraka's stage of puerile infatuation with the doctrine of Ron Karenga known as Kawaida. Kawaida stressed seven principles of a value system called the Nguzo Saba, and Baraka treats the system in *A Black Value System.* But the actions and writings of the Kawaida phase belong to a history of black sects and cults. Baraka now finds this stage singularly uninteresting.
14. Imamu Amiri Baraka, "The Congress of Afrikan People: A Position Paper," *Black Scholar* 6 (January 1975):9.

15. Imamu Amiri Baraka, "Needed: A Revolutionary Strategy," *Black Scholar* 7 (October 1976):45. For those who wish to pursue Baraka's most recent writings *Hard Facts* (a collection of poems written between 1973 and 1975) is available from Peoples' War, P.O. Box 663, Newark, N.J.

Chapter V: Critical Change and Blues Continuity

1. "Toward Guinea: For Larry Neal, 1937–1981." In *Spirit Run* (Detroit: Lotus Press, 1982). The present writer authored the volume.

2. Larry Neal, "Into Nationalism, out of Parochialism," *Performance* 2 (1972):95–96.

3. Ibid., p. 96. See also: Larry Neal, "The Black Contribution to American Letters: Part 2, The Writer as Activist — 1960 and After," in *The Black American Reference Book,* ed. Mabel Smythe (Englewood Cliffs, N.J.: Prentice-Hall, 1976), p. 779.

4. Larry Neal, review of *Shadow and Act* by Ralph Ellison, *Liberator* 4 (1964):28.

5. Larry Neal, "The Cultural Front," *Liberator* 5 (1965):26–27.

6. Larry Neal, "The Black Writer's Role: Richard Wright," *Liberator* 5 (1965):20. Subsequent citations are marked by page numbers in parentheses.

7. Larry Neal, "The Black Writer's Role: Ralph Ellison," *Liberator* 6 (1966):9–11. Subsequent citations are marked by page numbers in parentheses.

8. Larry Neal, "The Black Musician in White America," *Negro Digest* 16 (1967):55.

9. Larry Neal, "The Black Arts Movement," *The Black Aesthetic,* ed. Addison Gayle, Jr. (New York: Doubleday, 1971), pp. 272–90. Subsequent citations are marked by page numbers in parentheses.

10. Larry Neal, "Ellison's Zoot Suit," in *Ralph Ellison: A Collection of Critical Essays,* ed. John Hersey (Englewood Cliffs, N.J.: Prentice-Hall, 1974), pp. 58–79. The essay originally appeared in *Black World* 20 (1970):31–50. Subsequent citations are marked by page numbers in parentheses.

11. Neal, "Into Nationalism," p. 102.

12. Ibid. Subsequent citations are marked by page numbers in parentheses.

13. Neal, "Black Contribution to American Letters." Subsequent citations from the essay are marked by page numbers in parentheses. The analysis that follows first appeared in my 1981 essay "Generational Shifts."

14. Larry Neal, "Cultural Nationalism and Black Theatre," *Black Theatre* 1 (1968):9. Subsequent citations are marked by page numbers in parentheses.

15. Larry Neal, "Any Day Now: Black Art and Black Liberation," in *Black Poets and Prophets,* ed. Woodie King and Earl Anthony (New York: Mentor, 1972), p. 152.

16. Larry Neal, "Some Reflections on the Black Aesthetic," in *Black Aesthetic,* p. 13.

17. "Aesthetics and Culture: A View by Larry Neal," *The Drum* 9 (1978):11–12.

18. Neal, "Any Day Now," p. 152.

19. Ibid.

Chapter VI: An Editor from Chicago

1. Readings, articles and essays began to appear in journals and newspapers in the United States as early as the late sixties.

2. Black civic and academic leaders such as Roy Wilkins and Arthur P. Davis viewed an emergent Black Power generation with grave reservations.

3. Brooks conducted writers workshops in her own home in Chicago, and Kent both taught Afro-American literature courses at the University of Chicago and worked with the Organization of Black American Culture in Chicago.

4. Hoyt Fuller, "Towards a Black Aesthetic," in *The Black Aesthetic,* ed. Addison Gayle, Jr. (New York: Doubleday, 1971), pp. 3–12.

5. David Levering Lewis, *When Harlem Was In Vogue* (New York: Knopf, 1981), p. 48.

6. Etheridge Knight, "For Black Poets Who Think of Suicide," *Belly Song* (Detroit: Broadside, 1973), p. 45.

7. Ralph Ellison, *Invisible Man* (New York: Vintage, 1972), p. 136.

8. Stanley Fish, *Is There a Text in This Class?* (Cambridge: Harvard, 1982), p. 239.

9. Zora Neale Hurston, *Mules and Men* (New York: Perennial, 1970), p. 23.

Conclusion

1. T. S. Eliot, "Tradition and the Individual Talent," *Selected Essays* (New York: Harcourt, 1950), p. 10.

2. Barbara Herrnstein Smith, *On the Margins of Discourse* (Chicago: University of Chicago Press, 1978).

3. See Houston A. Baker, Jr., *Racial Poetry and State Philosophy,* Occasional Paper 12 (Minneapolis: Center for Humanistic Studies, University of Minnesota, 1986).

4. Gaston Bachelard, *The Poetics of Space* (Boston: Beacon, 1969).

5. LeRoi Jones, *The Autobiography of LeRoi Jones Amiri Baraka* (New York: Freundlich, 1984). All citations refer to this edition.

6. Eric Williams, *Capitalism and Slavery* (New York: G. P. Putnam, 1966).

7. Frederick Douglass, *Narrative of the Life of Frederick Douglass* (New York: Penguin, 1982), p. 107.

8. Richard Wright, *Black Boy* (New York: Perennial, 1966), p. 282.

Index

Aesthetics/aestheticism: disinterested, 14; and ethics, 151; new criticism on, 11; nineteenth-century, 11; of silence, 106, 107. *See also* Black Aesthetic

Africa, 4, 28, 68, 157, 167; past in, 26, 154

Afro-Americans. *See* Blacks

Angelou, Maya, 9

Art, 92; as agent of change, 51-52, 53; based on experience, 122-23; as change, 143, 156; and consciousness, 106; function of, 147, 155; ideology of race in, 154-55; independence in, 59; jazz as, 150; and politics, 151; as product and producer, 13; as propaganda, 51; serious, 122-23; theater as, 150-52. *See also* Black Art

Autobiography: Baraka's, 133, 172, 173, 174; in critical theory, 170-72

Bachelard, Gaston, 171

Baker, Houston A. Jr.: Black Aestheticism of, 142; on blues, 143; on *Cane*, 15-16; *The Journey Back* of, 141; *Modernism and the Harlem Renaissance* of, 3-4, 5-6, 172; on Neal, 159; *Singers of Daybreak* of, 16; *Workings of the Spirit* of, 3

Bakhtin, Mikhail, 170

Baldwin, James, 9, 95, 131

Ballads, 78-79

Baraka, Amiri (LeRoi Jones), 6, 13, 35, 49, 111-39, 164; on art based on experience, 122-23; autobiography of, 133, 172, 173, 174; on being black in America, 122, 123, 124; on black art, 113, 130, 131; *Black Art* of, 135, 136-37; *Black Fire* coedited by, 113, 140, 142; on black literature, 122, 123-24; on black manifest destiny, 136, 137; *A Black Mass* of, 131, 132; on black music, 122, 123; on black nationalism, 122, 130-31, 135, 137, 138-39; in black politics, 138; black power movement affects, 116; on black separatism, 122; on black sovereign state, 121-22; compared to Baldwin, 131; compared to William Carlos Williams, 133; "Courageousness" of, 16; *The Dead Lecturer* of, 111, 128-30, 132-33; *Dutchman* of, 125-26, 127, 151; *Experimental Death Unit #1* of, 131, 132; on freedom, 121-22, 126; Fuller on, 112; *Great Goodness of Life* of, 131; Harlem Black Arts Repertory Theatre School established by, 111, 130, 132, 145; heroes influence, 173-74; *Home, Social Essays* of, 120-25, 130; *Jello* of, 131, 132; on liberalism, 121; *Madheart* of, 131; on Malcolm X, 130; as Marxist, 138,

"A stunning critical achievement." —Henry Louis Gates, Jr.

When Houston A. Baker, Jr., one of America's foremost literary critics, first published *Afro-American Poetics* in 1988, it was hailed as a major revisionist history of both African American culture and criticism. Now available in paperback, this ambitious book juxtaposes two of the most fertile periods of African American culture, the 1920s and the 1960s; it includes essays on Jean Toomer, Countee Cullen, Amiri Baraka, Larry Neal, and Hoyt Fuller. This is also Baker's most personal book, tracing his beginnings as a scholar of Victorian literature, his "second birth" as he began teaching African American literature, and his visions and revisions of a black aesthetic.

"Baker's is a fascinating portrait of the literary critic as blues artist, reconstructing the products of two amazingly fruitful decades of engagement with Afro-American expressive culture in illuminating autobiographical examinations of his own—and indeed, Afro-American criticism's—momentous changes over that period of time."
—Michael Awkward, University of Michigan

"Readers who do not know much about black American literature would learn a great deal from *Afro-American Poetics*; those who do would be further enlightened."
—Peter Nazareth, *World Literature Today*

"For this student of black literature, the final impact of *Afro-American Poetics* is overwhelming. We now have the beginnings of a superstructure upon which to gauge individual pieces of black literature." —Eugene Kraft, *Callaloo*

Houston A. Baker, Jr., is professor of English, Albert M. Greenfield Professor of Human Relations, and director of the Center for the Study of Black Literature and Culture at the University of Pennsylvania. His many books of criticism include *Modernism and the Harlem Renaissance* and *Blues, Ideology, an Afro-American Literature*, and he has published three collections of poems.

Winner of the 1989–90 College Language Association Award For Outstandi Scholarship.

The University of Wisconsin Press
114 N. Murray Street, Madison, Wisconsin 53715

Cover illustration: Palmer Hayden, *The Subway,* c. 1930. Oil on canvas, 31 x 26 1/2". The State of New York / Adam Clayton Powell, Jr., State Office Building Collection.

Cover design: Nighthawk Design

ISBN 0-299-11504-6

9 780299 115043

9000